THE SONJO OF TANGANYIKA

Gateway of a Sonjo village

The Sonjo of Tanganyika

AN ANTHROPOLOGICAL STUDY OF AN
IRRIGATION-BASED SOCIETY

ROBERT F. GRAY

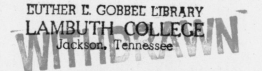
Published for the
INTERNATIONAL AFRICAN INSTITUTE
by the
OXFORD UNIVERSITY PRESS
LONDON NEW YORK TORONTO
1963

Oxford University Press, Amen House, London E.C.4

GLASGOW   NEW YORK   TORONTO   MELBOURNE   WELLINGTON
BOMBAY   CALCUTTA   MADRAS   KARACHI   LAHORE   DACCA
CAPE TOWN   SALISBURY   NAIROBI   IBADAN   ACCRA
KUALA LUMPUR   HONG KONG

Printed in Great Britain

To My Mother
and the Memory of My Father

PREFACE

This book is based upon field work which was carried out during the last six months of 1955. The meagre information about the Sonjo which I possessed prior to this visit indicated that they were a distinctive, closely knit society practising irrigation. I planned my research with the limited object of investigating the irrigation system and its relation to the social structure, hoping thereby to obtain insight into a type of ecology and social system which has not previously been studied in sub-Saharan Africa. In the present book I submit my findings and interpretations.

The period of my field research coincided with the dry season, during which the motor road to Sonjo is open. It was also the period during which the irrigation system was in full operation. I was fortunate in being able to witness the two important annual festivals of the Sonjo. Although the harvest festival was only celebrated at one village during my stay, the second festival took place at all the villages. Much of my information about Sonjo religion comes from observations and conversations at these festivals.

The Sonjo are quite definitely xenophobic in their attitude towards the outside world; some of the reasons for this will appear in the text of the book. In the past, the Sonjo villages have been virtually closed to outsiders, except for government officials, unless accompanied by an approved escort. My wife and I were not allowed to locate our camp inside any of the villages, and in the early weeks of research my movements in the villages were somewhat restricted and constantly observed. Later on, the suspicion with which I was first regarded decreased considerably. It was a great advantage during my first month to have as guide and informant Simon Ndula, the author of the mythological text, published by Fosbrooke (1955), which is discussed in chapter VII. He was a native Sonjo, seconded from his duties as government messenger and assigned to me by the District Commissioner of Masai District.

Our field camp was located near the villages of Kheri and

Ebwe—about a quarter of a mile from either village—and most of my observations were made at those two villages. The headman of Ebwe was unusually helpful. It was only through his sympathetic support that I was enabled to complete a house-to-house survey of an entire ward of that village. As regular informants I employed two very able young men, one from Kheri and the other from Soyetu. I made regular visits to Soyetu, spending about one day a week at that village. Most of my data were confirmed by informants from Kheri, Soyetu, and Ebwe. For the other three villages (there are six in all) my data are incomplete. Therefore, the statements in the text can be taken to apply to three of the villages except where I indicate otherwise. I am quite satisfied, however, that the same basic institutions are present in all the Sonjo villages.

As there were no English-speakers among the Sonjo, I used Swahili as a medium of communication. This language is known by nearly all the younger adult men of the tribe and by a fair number of older men. It is becoming the custom for men of the warrior class to spend from two to four years in other parts of Tanganyika or Kenya working as migrant labourers or livestock traders, and there they learn Swahili—the lingua franca of East Africa. In the later stages of my work I supplemented Swahili with a basic vocabulary of Sonjo words. My informants acted as interpreters when I interviewed some of the old men who knew no Swahili. My wife became acquainted with three Sonjo women who had learned Swahili during prolonged residences with their husbands at Loliondo. From them she was able to obtain some information which was otherwise inaccessible to me. In the book I indicate the native names for various items of technical equipment. This is more for the sake of the ethnographic record than for any value it has in my analysis. Otherwise vernacular words are kept to a minimum and are used only when I think that English equivalents do not adequately express an idea, or in some cases to emphasize that an idea is embodied in a special word. Every Sonjo word is identified or defined when first used.

No general anthropological study of the Sonjo had been made prior to my field research. A number of writings which deal in one way or another with the Sonjo are mentioned in the book. In addition to these, two articles not cited in the text which provide some background material are a short account of the defensive measures of the Sonjo by Fosbrooke (1955a) and some notes on Sonjo land tenure by Griffiths (1940). In the chapters that follow I shall be presenting for the most part data collected by myself in the field.

Tulane University
New Orleans
December 1961

ACKNOWLEDGEMENTS

My field research was financed by a Ford Foundation research grant, administered by the Institute of Current World Affairs. To both of these organizations I wish to acknowledge my gratitude. I am also grateful to the International African Institute for financial assistance in the publication of this book.

The project was first suggested to me by Mr. H. A. Fosbrooke, then Senior Sociologist for the Tanganyika Government. As a former administrative officer, he had been stationed in the Sonjo area and possessed a general knowledge of the tribe. My wife and I made the Fosbrooke home near Arusha our headquarters in Tanganyika, and our debt to him for advice, help, and hospitality is considerable.

Because of the difficulty of access to the Sonjo area, the field work was only possible with the generous help and encouragement of the government officials of Northern Masai District. The District Commissioner, Mr. S. W. Frazer-Smith, M.C., arranged for the transportation of our camp equipment from Arusha and provided a guide to help us find the place and an informant for the initial stage of the research. The District Officers at Loliondo, Major Horace Reed and Mr. F. G. Finch, received us with open hospitality when we arrived at that outpost and gave us every possible assistance in carrying out our project. Grateful acknowledgement is made to these people for their aid.

Professor E. H. Winter went over my field notes with me and gave me valuable help in planning the book. Professor Fred Eggan and the late Professor Robert Redfield read most of the first draft and offered detailed criticisms and advice as well as encouragement. In the final draft I made a number of changes suggested by Professor Daryll Forde and Dr. John Middleton. My wife participated throughout in the making of this book, both as companion in the field and as consultant in the study. She typed draft after draft of the text without complaint. I wish to thank Mr. Frank Newsom for drawing the maps and diagrams in the book. The photographs were taken by myself.

My greatest single debt for this study is owed to those Sonjo individuals who, overcoming their initial instinctive suspicions, provided me with most of the data for my analysis, and in many instances showed us great personal kindness. Without the patient guidance of my informants—Ndula, Gidia, and Daniel —my attempt to understand the Sonjo social system would have come to naught.

CONTENTS

ILLUSTRATIONS

PLATES

Chapter I

INTRODUCTION

THE East African plateau receives so little rain over most of its plains and valleys that the climate, except at higher altitudes, is in many places critical for agriculture.[1] The Sonjo inhabit one of those regions which are too arid for the cultivation of crops by rainfall alone. The land, however, is well endowed with streams and springs which are favourably located so that their waters can be used for irrigation. The Sonjo make use of this water and are thus enabled to base their subsistence mainly upon crop cultivation. Now the practice of irrigation is unusual among the native societies of East Africa, and the Sonjo are perhaps the only group depending wholly upon it in their agriculture.[2] Moreover, certain social institutions of the Sonjo are unique in East Africa, and some of these appear to be specially adapted to an irrigation economy. The present study starts with the hypothesis, based upon these general observations, that Sonjo social structure is related in a significant way to the practice of irrigation. Therefore, in the following account of the Sonjo we shall focus on the ecological adaptation of the society, giving special attention to the irrigation system.

A second important factor affecting the Sonjo is their position vis-à-vis the Masai; for they are located in the interior of the large tract of country constituting the tribal territory of the Masai, and there form an enclave of Bantu agriculturalists surrounded by nomadic pastoralists who differ from them in language and culture. Both of these factors will be taken into account in analysing the social institutions of the Sonjo, but in different ways. The Masai factor will be dealt with mainly as a unique historical situation, because it is difficult to find close

[1] This is clearly indicated in the series of rainfall maps and charts in *East Africa Royal Commission Report* (1955).

[2] Three or four other tribes in East Africa have been reported as practising irrigation, but only as a supplement or alternative to rain crops. These will be discussed later.

parallels among other societies for comparison. The irrigation factor, however, is more amenable to comparative treatment, for irrigation is widely practised in different parts of the world, and a certain amount of research has been done on this subject. In the following analysis of Sonjo society, relevant theory will be used as a guide wherever possible.

THE SOCIOLOGY OF IRRIGATION

A basic assumption which will be adhered to throughout this study is that the geographical environment has a significant effect on the forms of organization of human society. This subject has been discussed at length by Forde (1934), who describes a series of societies in a variety of environmental situations. Guarding against the fallacy of geographical determinism, he states his conclusions cautiously:

> The habitat at one and the same time circumscribes and affords scope for cultural development in relation to the pre-existing equipment and tendency of a particular society, and to any new concepts and equipment that may reach it from without. (Forde 1934 : 464)

My assumption is compatible with these conclusions as far as they go, but it implies a firmer statement as to the relation between a society and its environment. Forde, although he describes several societies practising irrigation, does not analyse the special features distinguishing this type of adaptation.

Steward (1955) also deals with the question of environment and makes use of the concept of 'ecology', which he defines as 'an heuristic device for understanding the effect of environment on culture' (Steward 1955 : 30). This concept is implemented with a methodological programme for the study of ecology. The 'three fundamental procedures' which he lists are as follows:

> First the interrelations of exploitive or productive technology and environment must be analyzed. . . . Secondly, the behavior patterns involved in the exploitation of a particular area by means of a particular technology must be analyzed. . . . The third procedure is to ascertain the extent to which the behavior patterns entailed in exploiting the environment affect other aspects of culture. (Steward 1955 : 40–1)

Steward's concept of ecology is in accord with my own plan for the study of Sonjo society, and his programme of procedure will be followed in a general way in the analysis. However, I shall be stressing social structure, which is only a part of the socio-cultural whole that Steward deals with in the main. Therefore my application of the ecology concept will not be as extensive as his programme suggests.

Most of the research on irrigation-based societies has been concerned with the role played by irrigation in the rise of civilization, and since the Sonjo are a small tribal group with a primitive technology, this research has only limited relevance to our problem. Steward himself has undertaken an investigation of irrigation societies, but his preliminary report deals only with large complex societies which are much beyond the Sonjo in cultural development: this is a comparative study of developmental patterns in a series of some principal irrigation civilizations from both the Old World and the New World (Steward 1949). He bases his work on a theory of 'multilinear evolution', which he discusses at length in a later publication (Steward 1953). Irrigation societies, according to Steward, constitute one of several societal types, and their development represents only one of several lines of social evolution. He contrasts this viewpoint with the work of Childe, in which irrigation is represented, at least by implication, as a universal stage in the development of civilization (Childe 1946 : 83; 1954 : 24). Steward asserts that Childe's method has 'entailed a retreat into broad generalizations' and describes it as a 'heritage of nineteenth-century unilinear evolution' (Steward 1953 : 316).

The principal conceptual categories that Steward uses in his study of irrigation societies—formative and florescent periods of development, conquest, militaristic expansion, and the like—are not appropriate concepts to apply in the Sonjo study, which is essentially a synchronic analysis of a small tribal society about which we have little historical information of the kind that Steward uses. Since his data in this study are taken from history and archaeology he has little occasion to bring his own programme for ecological research, as quoted above, into operation. He recognizes the importance of analysing primitive stages of irrigation societies and makes some shrewd observations regarding the origins of irrigation; but in the absence of adequate data—archaeological or ethnological —these observations are essentially conjectures based on consideration of the environmental conditions and the probable technical equipment of the originating societies.

The environments [he writes] are arid or semi-arid, which, contrary to a common belief, did not impose great difficulties and thereby stimulate cultural development. Instead, they facilitated culture growth because they were easily tilled by digging-stick and irrigation farming. The tropical rain forests, the northern hardwood forests, and the sodded plains areas, on the other hand, were exploited only with the greatest difficulty by people who lacked iron tools. (Steward 1949 : 7)

Braidwood, in discussing the origin of civilization in the Near East from the viewpoint of archaeology, also makes some suggestions as to probable conditions in the early stages of an irrigation society. Thus he writes:

The point has already been suggested that social as well as economic factors are involved, even in the development of the elementary irrigation schemes we believe appeared in Ubaidan times. To make a large irrigation system efficient, a considerable amount of social control, a sense of land law and riparian rights, perhaps even a maintenance agency and police force, must have been available as well as technological know-how. (Braidwood 1952 : 39)

These thoughtful suggestions will be carried in mind as we proceed in our analysis of the Sonjo.

Steward's preliminary conclusions regarding developmental regularities in irrigation civilizations were later discussed and modified at a symposium of specialists on several of these irrigation societies (Steward *et al.* 1955). One of the participants at this symposium, who is a specialist in Chinese history, Karl Wittfogel, has studied irrigation societies in a broader context than the others, and we shall now consider his writings in some detail. His symposium paper (Wittfogel 1955) was concerned, like the others, with the problem of historical development of irrigation civilizations, and hence it is not pertinent to the

Sonjo study. However, I shall quote a comment on this paper
made by Ralph Beals because it underlines the conjectural
nature of much of Wittfogel's theory.

> Mr. Wittfogel's paper gives the impression that our detailed
> information concerning China is very much less than for Meso-
> potamia or Peru. This possibly incorrect conclusion arises because
> Mr. Wittfogel tends to cast his statements either in terms of what
> *possibly* may have occurred or what *probably* occurred. (Steward *et al*
> 1955 :53)

In two later publications, Wittfogel (1956, 1957) has undertaken a comprehensive analysis of irrigation-based societies,
which he terms 'hydraulic' societies or civilizations. In general
he finds that hydraulic societies have strong and despotic central
governments, of a type commonly associated with Oriental
states. This is the reason for the title of his recent book—
Oriental Despotism (1957)—upon which our discussion will be
centred. In this book he is concerned with two main problems,
only the second of which has a bearing on the Sonjo study.
The two problems are intermingled in the book but will be
discussed separately here. In the first place he defines 'oriental
despotism' and contrasts it unfavourably with the political institutions of western society. Since some of his despotic or
totalitarian societies are not based upon irrigation economies,
the role of the 'hydraulic' factor is not immediately apparent.
Therefore he develops an elaborate theory to explain how the
despotic trait was diffused, through conquest or otherwise,
from 'core' areas, where irrigation is actually practised, to
'marginal' and 'submarginal' zones of the 'hydraulic world',
which contain non-irrigating societies (Wittfogel 1957 : 161–
227). Russia, as a 'marginal' hydraulic society, is given special
attention in the book. Thus the despotic element in Tsarist
Russia, which has persisted or recurred in Russian governments
down to the present, is stated to have been introduced by the
Tartars (a people tinged with hydraulic despotism) who conquered Russia in the thirteenth century (Wittfogel 1957 : 219–
25).

Having established to his satisfaction that there is a close
correlation between despotic government and the practice of

irrigation, Wittfogel attempts to explain why this should be so by analysing the nature of a 'hydraulic' situation. This constitutes his second main problem—one which has relevance for the Sonjo study. His method is to state a proposition or hypothesis as to some characteristic of hydraulic societies, and then to adduce evidence drawn from a number of irrigation-based societies in support of the hypothesis. A large number of these hypotheses are presented, and some of them will be discussed later. The data which Wittfogel uses in his analysis are drawn primarily from large complex societies—particularly the irrigation-based civilizations of Egypt, Mesopotamia, India, Southeast Asia, and China—but he also cites data from contemporary tribal societies and implies that some, at least, of his generalizations apply to them as well (Wittfogel 1957 : 3). At an early point in the book he makes a distinction between very small-scale irrigation, which he terms 'hydroagriculture', and larger irrigation systems, which he terms 'hydraulic agriculture', and with which he is concerned in his analysis. Of the former he writes, 'it does not involve the patterns of organization and social control that characterize hydraulic agriculture and Oriental despotism' (Wittfogel 1957 : 18); but 'hydroagriculture' is not mentioned again in the book, nor is it anywhere clearly defined. As he frequently cites the Chagga of East Africa, the Pueblo Indians, and other tribal societies (which are roughly equivalent to the Sonjo in cultural and social development) he evidently regards them as practising 'hydraulic agriculture'. The Chagga, for example, are mentioned some thirty different times in illustrating a variety of characteristics of hydraulic societies, ranging from the building of 'huge defence structures' (p. 36) to the terrorism exercised by hydraulic governments (p. 142).

In this book Wittfogel seems to use the terms 'hydraulic civilization' and 'hydraulic society' interchangeably, and he does not clearly distinguish between 'primitive' and 'civilized' in applying his hypotheses to different irrigation societies. Neither does he discuss the problem of the origin and development of irrigation civilization, which was dealt with in the symposium (Steward et al. 1955). One of the major problems of the book appears to be to define the characteristics of hydraulic societies in general, and this problem should be pertinent to the Sonjo study. Wittfogel's failure to distinguish clearly between primitive and civilized societies in stating his hypotheses about the characteristic features of hydraulic societies makes it difficult to understand his intention as to the scope of application of the hypotheses. Moreover, since the hypotheses were formulated for the purpose of explaining his central theory —namely that hydraulic societies have despotic governments— they may be suspected of being biased so as to support the theory. Nevertheless, despite these shortcomings, Wittfogel's research represents the only attempt that has been made, so far as I know, to delineate the distinctive social features of irrigation-based societies, and as such it deserves careful consideration in planning a study such as this. Immediately following I have listed in brief form some of Wittfogel's hypotheses which seem to be pertinent to the situation of the Sonjo.

1. Water has specific qualities which distinguish it from all other natural resources. Its bulk, weight, and flowing properties require that it be moved by taking advantage of the law of gravity in leading it to lower levels. Human settlements must adjust themselves to these properties of water in relation to the terrain if they wish to use the water. Because of its bulkiness, the manipulation of all except the smallest sources of water supply creates a technical task which is solved either by mass labour or not at all (Wittfogel 1957 : 15).

2. The amount of water handled and the scale of the hydraulic works is related to the social organization of the hydraulic society. Thus a small source of water may be dealt with by a single family or a small group of neighbours, whereas a large quantity of water may require the organized mass labour of a large community (Wittfogel 1957 : 18).

3. Three types of hydraulic environments should be distinguished—arid, semi-arid, and humid. In an arid environment the existence of an agricultural society is wholly dependent on irrigation. Semi-arid environments may require irrigation as a supplement to rainfall in agriculture. In humid environments irrigation is usually practised as an alternative to rainfall farming because of preference for an aquatic plant, such as rice, as a crop. The social adaptations will differ according to the type of hydraulic environment (Wittfogel 1957 : 19).

4. Hydraulic economy has three paramount characteristics:

'Hydraulic agriculture involves a specific type of division of labour. It intensifies agriculture. And it necessitates co-operation on a large scale. . . . The first [characteristic] has been given practically no attention' (Wittfogel 1957 : 22).

5. Political leadership is identified with control of irrigation. This idea is present throughout the book. Wittfogel indicates that it is valid for simple tribal societies as well as larger societies, regardless of the nature of the political leadership. 'From the standpoint of the historical effect [he writes], it makes no difference whether the heads of a hydraulic government were originally peace chiefs, war leaders, priests, priest-chiefs, or hydraulic officials *sans phrase*' (Wittfogel 1957 : 27).

6. 'The hydraulic régime attaches to itself the country's dominant religion. . . . A dominant religion may have no competitors' (Wittfogel 1957 : 87).

These hypotheses have been selected, not because they are supported with adequate anthropological evidence: as a matter of fact they are not. Although Wittfogel has combed the anthropological literature quite thoroughly, the available data on irrigation are thin and inadequate. As an example, he cites the Suk of East Africa in nine different places although the information about Suk irrigation, which is relevant to his thesis, consists of exactly one line of text: 'Every male must assist in making the ditches under penalty of beating' (Beach 1911 : 15)! The hypotheses were selected because, as they are stated by Wittfogel, they are in some measure relevant to the anthropological task of analysing Sonjo society according to the ecological principles formulated by Steward. I shall keep them in mind during the course of the study, and when my data have all been presented I shall again consider them. General hypotheses of this kind, which assert certain social consequences from a certain type of economy, cannot be proved or disproved by the analysis of a single society; but if these hypotheses are in accord with my findings in this study they will have gained a limited validity, and at least a start will have been made in defining the generic features of small irrigation societies which distinguish them from non-irrigation societies.

SONJO ORIGINS AND HISTORY

In his classification of the Bantu languages, Guthrie (1948 : 43) groups the Sonjo and the Ikoma (to be discussed later) with a cluster of tribes located on the eastern shore of Lake Victoria. The largest and best known tribes of this group are the Ragoli and Gusii of Kenya and the Kuria of Tanganyika. In regard to the reliability of this classification, the Sonjo language is one of those which, according to Guthrie, 'have been grouped on the basis of the meager information contained in the word-lists, or a relationship asserted by some earlier writer has perforce been used. It will therefore be very likely that when more data become available a considerable modification

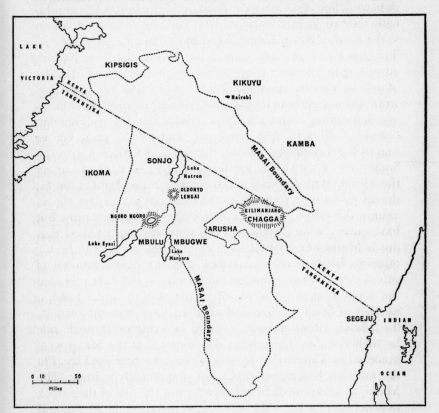

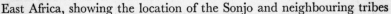

East Africa, showing the location of the Sonjo and neighbouring tribes

of the classification may be necessary in such cases' (p. 30). The author does not state the source of his information about the Sonjo, but in view of the above statement we cannot place much confidence in the position to which he assigns them in his classification. Some of the young men of the tribe who have travelled widely as migrant labourers and livestock traders have their own ideas about the linguistic affinities of the Sonjo. They state that linguistic communications are established more easily with the Meru of Mount Kenya (a tribe related closely to the Kikuyu) than with other Bantu tribes of northern Tanganyika or Kenya, and therefore postulate a close relationship between the two languages.

In racial classification likewise it is difficult from available data to define accurately the position of the Sonjo. Geographically they are located about midway between the three divisions of the Eastern Bantu distinguished by Seligman (1957 : 196–7). The Eastern Bantu are differentiated from the 'true Negro', according to Seligman (1957 : 162), by the 'infusion of Hamitic blood' in various amounts. The conditions of my own field work did not permit the gathering of anthropometric data, so my description is based only on visual inspection. The skin colour, medium to light brown, is of about the same hue as that of the Tanganyika Masai. There is less variation with the Sonjo—fewer dark skins are found among them than among the Masai. With few exceptions the Sonjo are slight in build; the heavy-set type, frequently seen in Masai groups, are absent among the Sonjo. They are below the Masai in stature but have quite a wide variation in this trait. It seems unlikely that much Masai blood could have entered the tribe. The hostile relations between the two tribes, and the Masai attitude of superiority and contempt for cultivators, would have excluded the Sonjo from access to Masai women. On the other hand, a number of Sonjo women and children have been adopted by the Masai, either through capture in raids or through sale by their families. There is good evidence that the Masai were preceded in Tanganyika by other groups of the same race. On this question Fosbrooke (1956 : 205) has recently written: 'The Masai, as we know them today, were not the first of their stock to penetrate; we know that the Kwavi preceded the Masai, and there is evidence that other groups preceded the Kwavi.' It is

quite possible that the physical traits of the Sonjo resembling
those of the Masai were implanted through mixture with some
of these earlier groups before the Masai arrived to make
contact with the Sonjo.

Historical traditions

The Sonjo elders are extraordinarily poor informants on
their own origins and past history. Their detailed knowledge
of past events goes back little farther than present memory can
reach. Two reasons can be discerned for this. In the first place
the people have almost a complete lack of interest in genealogies: there are no dynastic genealogies to provide a chronological framework for tribal history; an adult is seldom able
to trace his ancestors farther back than his grandparents, and
some elders did not know the names of their father's father.
Secondly, the tribal religion involves a series of myths to which
practically all historical traditions more than a generation or
two old have been assimilated. In this context, by 'myths' I
mean stories of the past which include supernatural elements.
Therefore we must consider these myths and see whether any
historical facts can be separated from them.

Sonjo mythology revolves around a culture hero named
Khambageu who, according to general belief, performed
miraculous acts, brought in a golden age of the Sonjo, was
ultimately deified, and now dwells in heaven near the summit
of Oldonyo Lengai mountain. The subject matter of these
myths will be discussed more fully in chapter VII; here it is
only necessary to indicate briefly their bearing on a reconstruction of Sonjo history. According to the myth that is most
often told, Khambageu first appeared at a village called Tinaga
which no longer exists. He was treated badly by the people of
Tinaga and finally retaliated by bringing disaster upon the
village. Many of the villagers died, and the survivors left the
village in two groups: one group, who were magically deprived
of their ability to speak the Sonjo language, migrated to Ikoma
and founded the tribe of that name. The others joined the Sonjo
village of Kheri, where their descendants live to this day as a
separate clan. Khambageu himself then came to the village of
Soyetu for a long stay, performing numerous miracles for the
welfare of the people and banishing sickness and hunger from

the tribe. He left Soyetu for a sojourn in a village called
Belwa, which no longer exists. Finally he came to the present
village of Rokhari, died, and ascended to heaven from there.
These basic events appear in all versions of the myth. The
villages of Rokhari and (to a lesser extent) Soyetu find in this
myth a charter for the superior ritual status which they enjoy
among the Sonjo villages. Further miraculous deeds of Khambageu occurred in other villages and are recounted in local
myths having currency in the villages concerned, but these are
poorly known, or not at all, in different villages.

These mythological events are believed to have taken place
in comparatively recent times when the tribe was constituted
more or less as at present. In fact Sonjo time perspective is
fantastically foreshortened, and people usually tell myths as if
they had happened in the days of their grandfathers, though
other evidence may indicate that the events took place eight
generations ago or longer. The chronology of the myths tends
to be contradictory. For example, in one group of myths
Khambageu is credited with founding several of the villages
and miraculously creating the springs which make them hab-
itable. But according to other myths he is supposed to have
visited these same villages for the first time and performed
miracles there when the villages were already going concerns.
There are some different myths concerning Khambageu which
are unrelated to the above and which seem to be known only
in fragmentary form. In these myths, Belwa and several other
abandoned villages are mentioned, but none of the present
villages.

If we assume an historical basis for the myths, it might be
argued that an unusual leader by the name of Khambageu
once appeared among the Sonjo at some time of crisis, perhaps
brought on by a failure of irrigation water or a disastrous attack by an enemy. The period when the Sonjo were first
seriously molested by the Masai could have constituted such
a crisis. The suggestion in the myths of old villages being
abandoned and new ones formed might indicate considerable
movement and readjustment within the tribe. When these
drastic events had run their course, a cult may have arisen
honouring the leader Khambageu, first as a culture hero and
magician, and ultimately as a god. Two chronological levels of

mythology can be distinguished, the first concerning Belwa and other extinct villages and the second starting with events in Tinaga and involving the present villages. It would be plausible to conclude that Khambageu was already a legendary figure before the present villages had been formed, and that his supposed activities in those villages are recent myths formulated during the course of his apotheosis.

Since Khambageu is a supernatural figure as well as a culture hero and is now regarded as a god—a statement for which I shall present further evidence in chapter VII—it would be incautious to draw inferences based on the assumption of his historical existence. However, I see no reason for suspecting that the place names occurring in the myths might have been invented. As the sites of these places are identified and explored in future research, the mythical events in which they are involved may suggest clues leading to a better understanding of early Sonjo history.

The site of Tinaga, which is the only abandoned village that I was able to visit, is about ten miles from the nearest existing village. It was laid out in much the same way as the present villages and appeared to possess an excellent water supply for irrigation. I could discover no clues as to the real cause of its abandonment, but it must have happened quite a long time ago for all memory of it to have been lost and for the myth of supernatural disaster to have been formed. The most important village mythologically is Belwa, which, like Khambageu himself, seems to have undergone an apotheosis; it is now thought of as located in heaven, or as synonymous with heaven. The name occurs in the invocation with which communal prayers are opened, in the phrase, '. . . open the sluices of Belwa', which is meant as a supplication for rain. According to my informants, the location of the ancient village of Belwa is unknown, but a District Officer, Grant (1953), has stated that the site is near Lake Magadi. Whatever the actual historical position of Belwa, it is now understood as a symbol of the Sonjo homeland and has been elevated to heaven in mythology.

It will be noted that the myths of Khambageu resemble the Gospel account of the life of Jesus in some points. These resemblances will be seen more clearly after the myths and ritual have been described in full in chapter VII. The elements of

similarity include a supernatural birth, the performing of
miracles of a compassionate nature, death following neglect and
mistreatment by the people, ascent to heaven, post-mortem
identification with God, and a promise of salvation for believers
who have undergone a specified initiation rite. Nothing resembling this complex of ideas is to be found in other East
African societies, so far as I have been able to discover. Therefore the beliefs must have developed independently among the
Sonjo, or else they were borrowed from a Christian source. If
we accept the latter explanation, it seems unlikely that the
beliefs could have been introduced by European missionaries.
In the first place the resemblances are only in the field of
general ideas and do not extend to names or detailed events.
Moreover, the evident antiquity of the Sonjo cult would seem
to antedate the earliest possible contact with Europeans. The
myths tell of the founding of villages and the creation of the
irrigation system. The ritual is highly developed and uniform
at all the villages. The priesthood is hereditary and must go back
a number of generations. In short, if certain elements in Sonjo
religion were borrowed from Christian sources, the contact must
have been very ancient and perhaps indirect. This question requires more research before a final conclusion will be possible.

Relations with other tribes

Both the Sonjo and Ikoma possess traditions of a common
origin, but the traditions exist in different versions in the two
tribes. The Sonjo version is incorporated in the myth of the
destruction of Tinaga, which was cited above. This event is
not conceived of as happening in the distant past, but only
about two generations ago. Although the Sonjo speak of the
Ikoma as being a 'brother' tribe they have little knowledge
about them. The fact that the Ikoma language is incomprehensible to the Sonjo is explained by reference to the myth
according to which the immigrants from Tinaga, who became
the Ikoma, lost their knowledge of the Sonjo language. The
Ikoma also recognize their common origin with the Sonjo but
place the parting far in the past.[1] According to their version,

[1] My information was obtained from informants during a four-day visit to
Ikoma for the purpose of investigating Sonjo-Ikoma relations. This was after I
had left the Sonjo, so I was not able to check these new data with Sonjo informants.

the parent tribe of the Sonjo and Ikoma inhabited a place called Regata, the location of which is not known. The Ikoma say they left Regata because of famine and migrated to their present home. Their name for the Sonjo is Abaregata. They are not familiar with the name Tinaga. The headman, named Makondo, of one of the six subsections of the tribe was able to recite the names of his ancestors through ten generations, going back to the founder of his clan, who is supposed to have been one of the original immigrants from Regata.

One trait common to both tribes is the peculiar custom of marking infants with scars under the left breast and over the left scapula. The Ikoma explain this custom by a medical theory which is essentially secular: a harmful black substance in the blood of infants, they say, must be drawn off in this way to protect the child's health. For the Sonjo the operation is a religious rite of initiation, originating with Khambageu and in some way comparable to baptism. The term *ntemi* is applied to the operation in both tribes. This word contains the root of the name by which the Sonjo call themselves as a tribe—*Batemi*. With the Ikoma the paramount chief has the title *motemi*, but the elders state that this office was first established under German rule. Previous to that time the ruling power of the tribe was a council composed of eight elders from each clan. In those days the members of the age-grade of senior warriors were called *abatemi*. The Germans, they say, appointed a chief and arbitrarily applied the term *motemi* to him.[1] The other linguistic and cultural evidence does not indicate a particularly close relationship. The basic vocabularies of the two tribes show marked differences. House types and methods of cultivation are quite different. The craft of basket-making is highly developed among the Ikoma and entirely absent from the Sonjo. With leather-working it is the other way round. There have been no active bonds between the two tribes for many generations at least. While the Sonjo and Ikoma have quite possibly descended from the same parent stock, the available evidence indicates that they separated a very long time ago.

The first European to contact the Sonjo was the German explorer, A. G. Fischer, who travelled through the region in

[1] The term *motemi* is used in four or five other East African tribes to designate 'chief' (Johnston 1919).

1883. He mentions them only in passing as 'an agricultural people, who are descended from the Wa-Segeju tribe settled on the coast near Tanga, and are said to have been driven many years ago into this Masai country in consequence of famine' (Fischer 1884 : 78). Fischer's theory of Sonjo origin was evidently accepted at the time, and the name 'Segeju' appears on some of the German maps of the region as an alternative to 'Sonjo' (e.g. Baumann 1894 : folding map, and Langhans). Oscar Baumann (1894 : 157), who explored near the Sonjo but did not actually contact the tribe, also mentions this theory. A geologist, Fritz Jaeger (1913 : 117), in a discussion of the geology of the region, devotes a page to a general description of the Sonjo villages and repeats the statement that the Sonjo are related to the Segeju.

The earliest published mention of the Sonjo seems to be in an article by T. Wakefield (1870), a missionary at Mombasa. On the basis of information obtained from a native of the northern Tanganyika coast, Sadi bin Ahedi, Wakefield describes the routes of native trading caravans from the coast to the interior of East Africa. Concerning the Sonjo he writes (p. 312):

Sadi says that the Wasonjo are Wasegeju immigrants, who left Shungwaya and came to this region, in which they have settled. (Shungwaya is a district between Goddoma and Kauma (Wanyika-land); and Sadi states that it was the original home of all the Wasegeju.)

This article is evidently the main source of Fischer's theory that the Sonjo are an offshoot of the Segeju.

I could find no evidence whatever in support of this theory. Intensive inquiry among the Sonjo failed to reveal any knowledge of the Segeju tribe or any tradition of having migrated from the coast. I later pursued the inquiry among the Segeju themselves, and again no tradition of relationship with the Sonjo was found, although the Segeju, unlike the Sonjo, have a keen interest in their own past and have traced back their history in some detail for several centuries (Baker 1949). The main body of the Segeju live in fishing villages along the coast, and now speak a dialect of Digo, as well as Swahili. One branch of the tribe, however, lives inland and uses a language which the people claim is the original Segeju (or Daiso) language. A vocabulary sample of this language when compared with Sonjo showed few cognates or other resemblances. The idea that a group of coastal people migrated into the arid interior of Masailand and created a new culture based on irrigation finds no support in cultural comparisons or in existing historical traditions in either tribe, and is inherently improbable. There is one similarity between the two tribes that I take to be independent responses to similar situations rather than indicating historical relationship: in both tribes the villages were fortified for protection against Masai raids. The Segeju villages were surrounded by walls of coral stone, while the Sonjo planted thorn hedges for this purpose. Fischer, who had lived on the coast for a long time and who was no doubt familiar with Segeju villages, may have given undue weight to this resemblance when he first contacted the Sonjo, and assumed a genetic relationship between the two tribes. It is also possible that Sadi bin Ahedi was influenced by this similarity when he informed Wakefield that the Sonjo were Segeju immigrants.

Still another suggestion as to the origin of the Sonjo is given by Dundas (1924 : 52), who relates them to the Chagga tribe inhabiting the slopes of Kilimanjaro. In discussing the history of the Kimaro and Wakimaha clans he tells how they rebelled against the chief Mkuruo and were defeated. 'Of those defeated by Mkuruo, it is related that they fled and settled North West of Mount Meru, where they remain to this day, and are known under the name of Sonjo.' From Dundas's account there is no way of dating this alleged event, and no other information has come to light which might confirm or reject the assertion. I was not able to investigate among the Kilimanjaro Chagga, but two Chagga teachers working with the Sonjo found the Sonjo language to be entirely incomprehensible. However, whether this particular tradition is correct or not, the Chagga also practise irrigation and it is not unlikely that the two tribes have at least inherited that culture complex from the same source. The Chagga irrigation system has been described by Gutmann (1926 : 413–21). It differs from the Sonjo system in that there are over a thousand separate channels, each of which is said to be controlled by a single clan, whereas a Sonjo irrigation system is under the communal control of a village composed of several clans. The two tribes have different types of social organizations, perhaps as the result of these differences in irrigation methods.

Other tribes in East Africa which have been reported as practising irrigation are the Suk and Marakwet of Kenya. About the Suk we have little information except that irrigation is practised and is important in the tribal economy. The description of the system by Beech (1911 : 15) only covers a few lines in its entirety. 'The irrigation system [he writes] is most ingenious, and its original construction must have required a vast amount of toil and patience. Irrigation ditches are the property of the tribe, not of the individual. Every male must assist in making the ditches under penalty of beating.' The Marakwet irrigation system has been described by Henning (1951 : 201–10) with considerable detail as to the physical and engineering features. According to Marakwet tradition, the furrows were already in existence when their forefathers came down from the north and settled in the country 'many generations ago' (Henning 1951 : 202). This author, however, tells us little about the social organization of the tribe or how the use of irrigation water is regulated.

Although in the present state of our knowledge it is impossible to state more precisely the genetic relations of the Sonjo with other East African Bantu tribes, we can investigate as a separate problem the history of the irrigation complex of the Sonjo. Two possible explanations come to mind as to the origin of the irrigation system. (1) It can be thought of as an independent invention of the forefathers of the present Sonjo. These people might have been subsisting precariously by cultivating rain crops and thus have been strongly motivated to develop irrigation systems once the idea occurred to them. There are serious difficulties in the way of accepting this theory. First we would have to assume that the climate was wetter than it is now, or else even precarious rain-farming would have been impossible. Furthermore, it hardly seems justified to posit independent invention in the case of a radical change in methods of agriculture—such as the adoption of irrigation represents—if reasonably plausible evidence of borrowing can be adduced. (2) A second explanation would assert that the precursors of the Sonjo already possessed knowledge of irrigation when they settled in the Sonjo valleys and constructed the irrigation systems that still exist. There is nothing inherently improbable in this theory, and the empirical evidence that we possess supports it.

Irrigation in East African prehistory

Wakefield (1870), in the article referred to above, describes a mountain named Kiti which was located somewhere near the Sonjo area. Of the inhabitants of the mountain he writes (pp. 312–13):

Wa-Ngurumani (some call them Wa-Utimi, and others, Wa-Baghasi, but Sadi says the first is the proper name) live on the top. There is water on the summit (a spring), which is perennial. The people cultivate the ground, and make trenches or channels, by which water is conducted in various directions to the plantations.

Although I cannot identify this mountain for certain, it is very probable that the settlement referred to was a Sonjo village which has since been abandoned. In any case, considering the date of publication and the source of information, this passage provides clear evidence that irrigation was practised in the region of the present Sonjo at least one hundred years ago.

The fact that at least four different tribes in the area now practise irrigation suggests either that the trait has diffused from one tribe to the other, or that they have all inherited the trait from an ancient irrigation culture in East Africa. This second hypothesis has some evidence in its support which we shall now review. Fosbrooke (1953 : 63) has reported the existence of several massive earth dams in Masai District which were evidently built to create large ponds of surface water. One of these is visible from the steep road running from the rim of Ngorongoro Crater down to the Balbal Depression. He also mentions ingeniously constructed wells at several points in the district. These hydraulic works are much more eleborate than anything attempted by the Masai themselves in historic times, and indicate the presence of a proto-historical people with a high level of technical skill in water control. A deep

c

well at Ngassumat in South Masailand, described briefly by
Koenig (1951 : 53–4), was built with a ramp, containing stone
steps and protected by limestone walls, leading down to near
the water level of the well. It is still used by the Masai for
watering cattle. The wells were evidently built by a pastoral
people with better capacity for co-ordinating their labour than
the Masai. The purpose of the dams is not so readily apparent,
but they were probably meant to impound water for watering
livestock during the dry season.

More pertinent for our problem are some ruins at Engaruka,
where there is clear evidence of a prosperous population which
practised agriculture under irrigation. This site, which has
been described by Leakey (1936), is located in the Rift Valley
of northern Tanganyika about sixty miles from the nearest
Sonjo village. The remains include stone walls and building
sites and a series of irrigation terraces which, as Leakey estimates, must have supported a population of between thirty
and forty thousand. The water available for irrigation today
is only sufficient for a small community of about 200 people,
and it is quite likely that the prehistoric town was abandoned
because of a decrease in the water supply, perhaps caused by
tectonic movements which are not uncommon in this volcanic
region. H. A. Fosbrooke who has inspected the Engaruka ruins
states in a recent publication (1957 : 325) that 'there are points
in Sonjo culture suggesting that they were picked up from
Engaruka. The position of the villages, the terraced house sites
and paths, the stone fireplaces and the irrigation system are
examples of this.' In this article there is reproduced an aerial
photograph of part of the Engaruka site.

Engaruka is not well known to the present Sonjo and I
failed to find any traditions, mythical or otherwise, linking
them with the site. This is understandable, because the Sonjo
did not travel freely through Masailand before European law
and order was imposed and reduced the danger of Masai
attack. It is possible that the inhabitants of Engaruka were ancestors of the Sonjo, and that the place may be the site of the
mythical village of Belwa; but if this is so, memory of it seems
to have been lost. The Ikoma have a word, *abagaruka*, meaning
'elders', which may be derived from the same root as Engaruka, and thus link them historically with the prehistoric town.

As yet only a preliminary survey of the site has been published. More exploration of the region is needed, and especially more archaeological excavation, before the significance of these ruins for Sonjo history can be assessed.

A few other reports of remains interpreted as ancient hydraulic works have come from East Africa. Wilson (1932 : 252) states that 'throughout Abyssinia, Uganda, Kenya, Tanganyika and part of Northern Rhodesia there are remains of an ancient system of terracing and irrigation'. His map of these finds shows a very extensive distribution indeed, but he admits the possibility that some of his 'terraces' may be due to natural causes or represent parallel cattle tracks on hillsides. Huntingford has reported what he interprets as ancient 'dikes' near Eldoret in Kenya. 'They consist of U or V-shaped depressions running generally across the slopes of ridges. . . . They seem to be more like dikes or ditches than roads' (Huntingford 1931 : 42). Three of these features are described, and he gives cross-sectional sketches to show their construction. In a more recent publication, Worsley and Rumberger (1949) describe a series of terraces along the Lyandembela River in the Uhehe region of southern Tanganyika. 'They consist of banks of earth varying in size around 20 yards by 5 yards, and divided by ditches about 3 feet deep and 4 feet wide' (42). This area is uninhabited at present and the nearby Wahehe have no knowledge of the builders. If the river were only a little higher than it is now, the authors reason, it would flood the terraces. They state their interpretation thus: 'It would seem to indicate a large labour force, presumably well organized and directed, at a time when the rivers were much larger or more liable to extensive flooding than today' (44). All these reports are concerned with accidental surface finds which were investigated only by visual inspection. No excavation has been done to determine even the simplest elements of material culture associated with the earth works. We have conclusive evidence in the ruins of Engaruka —and presumptive evidence elsewhere—that irrigation was practised in East Africa at an early date, probably before the present Bantu inhabitants had arrived on the scene. This is about all that can be safely said until systematic surveys and excavations have been made at the sites.

If this interpretation should be borne out in future research, it would be natural to look for a connexion between the ancient hydraulic culture of Tanganyika and the protohistoric cultures of Southern Rhodesia, which are better known. The Zimbabwe ruins and other monumental stone works have been studied by a number of investigators. Since the Zimbabwe problem is only remotely related to the present study, a survey of the extensive literature on the subject is not warranted here. A recent publication by Paver (1957) summarizes the present state of this research and gives a classified bibliography of the relevant literature. The Rhodesian finds that particularly concern us are in the Inyanga area east of Salisbury and above the escarpment overlooking Portuguese East Africa. A complex of walls, cisterns, and other structures of stone have been discovered there as well as vast areas of terraced hillsides, with much of the terracing constructed with stone retaining-walls. These ruins extend over an area of several thousand square miles. Summers (1958) has recently completed an investigation of the Inyanga site and published a detailed report of his findings. He describes systems of 'water furrows' and terraces which in most instances can hardly be anything else but irrigation systems. However, he leaves this interpretation open to doubt because of the fact that the present rainfall in the area appears to be sufficient for agriculture without the need of irrigation (Summers 1958 : 240). It appears to me that the evidence for irrigation at Inyanga is just as strong as at Engaruka. There is a remarkable and detailed similarity in aerial photographs of the two sites published by Summers (1958 : Plate I) and Fosbrooke (1957 : 324, Figure 10).

In summary, there is ample evidence that irrigation was widely known in Eastern Africa in ancient times. It is reasonable to conclude that the Sonjo (as well as other tribes now practising irrigation) have inherited this knowledge, either as the direct descendants of the ancient hydraulic society or as newcomers who have borrowed the art of irrigation from their predecessors. It will be difficult to decide between these two alternative hypotheses until archaeological excavation has revealed something about the culture of the early irrigating societies. From our present superficial knowledge, it would appear that Engaruka is a promising site at which to start this investigation.

Sonjo-Masai relations

In an analysis of the Masai age-group system, Fosbrooke (1956 : 194) establishes an association between the Merishari age-set and a battle fought at Manyara (about 100 miles south of the Sonjo), and dates the event at 1811. Although this is the earliest definite chronological landmark that we possess, it would seem reasonable to suppose that the vanguard of the Masai, in their southward migration, had reached the Sonjo at least a half-century earlier, in which case the two tribes would have been in contact for over 200 years.

The Masai, being pastoral nomads with a traditional contempt for agriculturalists, were regarded by the Sonjo as their enemies *par excellence*. But that their hostility was tinged with admiration is evident both in their expressed attitude towards the Masai and in the number of culture traits that they borrowed from them, particularly in the field of military affairs. As we shall see in chapter VI the Sonjo have adopted a number of Masai traits in their age-grade system. The costumes of the warriors are modelled after Masai costumes, though with significant variations. The fighting methods of the two tribes, however, were quite different. Whereas the Masai used the throwing spear, the Sonjo relied almost entirely on bows and poisoned arrows. Their relative weakness in numbers made it impossible for them to stand up against the Masai in open battle. Masai spears, captured in raids, were used as weapons by the Sonjo only in guarding the fortified gates of the villages in time of attack. When Masai warriors swept down on the villages, the Sonjo retired inside their fortified villages and held off the Masai by shooting their dreaded arrows. The Sonjo fields were outside the village and therefore vulnerable to destruction. According to the Sonjo, the Masai burned the standing crops in some of their early raids. In retaliation the Sonjo sent groups of warriors to attack the Masai camps at night. Showers of poisoned arrows were sent into the cattle kraal, killing large numbers of animals. Finally the two tribes agreed on a treaty whereby the Masai promised to leave the Sonjo crops alone and the Sonjo refrained from the wanton killing of Masai cattle.

Very likely the Sonjo once raised cattle, as their historical tradition claim. They explain their present lack of cattle as

owing to a prohibition by their deified hero Khambageu, but
in reality it must have been the advent of the Masai which
made cattle-raising unfeasible. Cattle would have been too
tempting to the predatory Masai and too easy to plunder. Thus
the Sonjo were reduced to keeping only goats. Sonjo institutions
were indirectly affected by the Masai in a number of ways.
They were isolated by them from kindred tribes for a long
period of time, and were forced to live in compact defensible
settlements. They were required to create an efficient military
organization and integrate it with a social structure that was
oriented primarily for the operation of an economy based on
an intricate irrigation system.

The Masai, for their part, seemed to respect Sonjo religion,
and certain Sonjo festivals were the occasions for a truce in
the otherwise hostile relations that prevailed between the two
tribes. Masai would often attend these festivals as individuals,
bringing offerings and requesting formal blessings from the
Sonjo God, especially children which seem to be scarce and
desperately wanted among the Masai. This is still done by the
Masai and was witnessed during my stay in the field. The
symmetrical cone of the 11,000-foot active volcano, Oldonyo
Lengai, is honoured by both Sonjo and Masai as a dwelling
place of God. Both the Masai name for the mountain (Oldonyo
Lengai) and the Sonjo name (Mogongo jo Mugwe) have the
same meaning—'Mountain of God'. Although the available
evidence is not conclusive, it seems likely that this idea originated with the Sonjo and that the Masai borrowed it when they
arrived in the region and established contact with the Sonjo.
The mountain is visible from all the Sonjo villages.

Chapter II

GEOGRAPHICAL SETTING OF VILLAGES

THE Sonjo, numbering about 4,500 in population,[1] occupy
six villages[2] which are located in the interior of Masai
District in northern Tanganyika near the Kenya border.
From Lake Natron, one of the large salt lakes of the Rift
Valley, the land rises westward, first abruptly up the Bast escarpment, which here forms the western wall of the Rift
Valley, and then more gradually to Loliondo sixty miles west.
The Loliondo highlands form the divide of the region: drainage
to the west flows to Lake Victoria, while the streams to the
east flow to Lake Natron. The Sonjo villages are about midway
between Loliondo and Lake Natron. The most northern village
is ten miles from the Kenya border. The villages are all built
on the slopes of escarpments which roughly form the margin
of a shallow depression about twenty miles in diameter. The
elevation of the villages varies around 5,000 feet above sea level.

The topography of northern Masai District presents a
variety of features ranging from well-watered mountains to
desert. In the south of the region, centring on the Ngorongoro
Crater, there is a cluster of tall volcanic mountains—Tanganyika's 'Giant Craterland'. The most northerly of these
volcanoes is Oldonyo Lengai, which has been active several
times in recent years. Its summit is visible from all the Sonjo
villages, and it has special religious significance for them,
as was explained above. Extending west and north from
these mountains is the elevated Serengeti Plain—a vast
stretch of undulating grasslands rising in parts to 6,000

---

[1] The figures from the 1957 census give the total as 4,388. The sex breakdown
gives a total for females of 2,325 and for males 2,063. I am assuming that the sex
ratio should be more nearly equal, and that some of the men who are away as
migrant labourers were not counted in the census.

[2] Village populations were not recorded in the census returns. I shall give some
estimates later in discussing individual villages.

feet. The Serengeti reaches westwards all the way to Lake
Victoria; on the east and north-east it is bounded by a series
of ridges which separate it from the Rift Valley and from the
Sonjo area. Northwards, as the Kenya border is approached,
the land rises to the Loliondo highlands. East of the Sonjo the
country is very rough as it descends some 3,000 feet to Lake
Natron. Rainfall in this whole area is considered insufficient
for agriculture except on the higher mountain slopes. Outside
the Sonjo tribal area, the land is only used by the Masai as

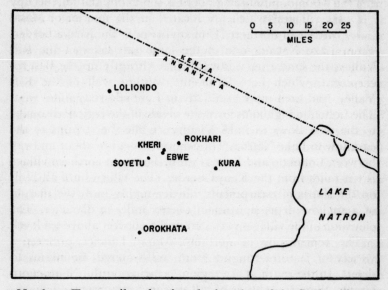

Northern Tanganyika, showing the location of the Sonjo villages

pasture for their livestock under a system of transhumance.
Large numbers of wild animals share the grass with the Masai
herds. Away from the mountains permanent waters are very
scarce, so that during the dry season the plains are deserted
by both Masai and antelopes.

Within this essentially pastoral milieu the Sonjo form an
enclave of Bantu agriculturalists, markedly different in their
way of life from the surrounding Masai. Their nearest Bantu
neighbours are the Ikoma, whose territory starts eighty miles to
the west across the Serengeti Plain. The Bantu Wambugwe and

Arusha of Tanganyika and the Nilo-Hamitic Kipsigis of Kenya, also agriculturalists, all live over a hundred miles away. Thus cut off from external trade and from the stimulation of friendly intercourse with other peoples for a long period of time—perhaps two centuries—the Sonjo were thrown back on the resources of their own society and environment. Their economy, based on agriculture and goat-herding, was almost self-sufficient. Iron, never plentiful among the Sonjo, was the only important commodity that had to be imported. It was obtained by barter from the Masai smiths. Salt was obtained from Lake Natron, as it is today. Gourds, which are used as milk and water containers, were raised by small colonies of Sonjo who settled, often temporarily for that special purpose, at the swampy estuaries of the streams entering Lake Natron. All other raw materials necessary for existence were found in the near vicinity of the villages. No doubt as a result of their enforced isolation, the Sonjo remained archaic in their technology and developed social and religious institutions which differed in a number of features from other East African societies.

A rain gauge is maintained at the government court building near the village of Ebwe, and records have been kept for eight years. According to these data, the average annual rainfall for the eight years is 18·75 inches. In only one year did it exceed 30 inches, and in two years 20 inches. The lowest total recorded was 12·02 inches. In view of the existing climatic conditions, this rainfall is below the minimum requirements for the successful cultivation of rain crops.[1] The distribution of rainfall over the year is quite variable according to the eight-year record. The two months of July and August were virtually free of rain. Three other months—June, September, and October —had only a trace of moisture in an average year. The planting of rain crops starts in January and February with the expectation that substantial rains will start at that time and continue through May. There is always uncertainty, though, and only the two months of January and April had rain on all the eight recorded years. Supplementary irrigation is customarily applied to these rain crops, but the supply of water for irrigating these

[1] *East Africa Royal Commission* (1955 : 252–5). In this report the minimum rainfall for growing rain crops in East Africa is set at from 20 to 30 inches, depending on other climatic conditions.

fields, as will be explained in chapter IV, fluctuates with the rainfall; therefore a dry year means poor crops, irrigation notwithstanding. The springs supplying water for irrigating the dry-season crops are much less subject to fluctuation. The significant point in the hydrology of the region is that the streams from the Loliondo highlands flow past the Sonjo area on their way to Lake Natron. The largest of these streams flows through the cultivated valley of one of the villages (Kura) and is the sole source of irrigation water. The other villages rely on streams for only part of their water. The valleys cultivated by these villages lie well below the general level of the land. At the base of the escarpment rising above the valleys there is a spring line whose springs produce the major portion of the irrigation water.

Except for the rain gauge, no other meteorological records are kept at Sonjo. During my stay, which coincided with the dry season, the days were hot but the nights were usually cool. The mornings would often become uncomfortably hot until midday, when the heat was tempered by a wind from the north, sometimes blowing so strongly that tent pegs would be pulled out of the ground.

The Sonjo tribal area is rather difficult of access from the nearest population centres or the main roads. Starting from Arusha, the government headquarters of Northern Province, a good road goes as far as Ngorongoro. From there to Loliondo, 120 miles north, the Serengeti Plain must be crossed by a rough track which is not considered passable by ordinary passenger cars. From the small government post at Loliondo it is only fifteen miles by foot to the nearest Sonjo village, but the car track is fifty miles over extremely rough country, and it quickly becomes impassable after a rain. The area can also be approached from Kenya by a road running from Narok to Loliondo which is passable in dry weather by trucks and Jeep-type vehicles. Because of the unsettled conditions in that part of Kenya due to the Mau Mau emergency, this road was seldom used in 1955. The Sonjo villages are connected by motor tracks, but as outside visitors are rare there is little traffic over them. The District Officer comes from Loliondo about once a month for administrative purposes, and the Sikh owner of the local shop drives in several times a year with a load of goods from his main shop at Loliondo. At other times the Sonjo are left to themselves, except for a very occasional visit by a government official, a hunter, or anthropologist.

THE VILLAGES

The topographical situations of all the Sonjo villages are remarkably similar. Built on the rocky slope of an escarpment, each village overlooks a small valley of cultivated fields. Beyond the valley the land rises gently to an uneven plain consisting of grasslands and light thorn bush with patches of acacia forest. Here the Sonjo graze their flocks of goats and sheep. In some cases the pastures of one village adjoin those of another. Behind the village the scarp rises steeply and is covered with heavier bush and forest. The orientation of the village is towards the valley and plain, though the forest is also exploited for wood and medicinal plants and the honey of wild bees. The village sites were obviously chosen with a view to their defensibility.

If the six villages are plotted on a map they appear to be located on the perimeter of a rough semicircle. Four of them are spaced fairly close together on a ten-mile line running north-east and south-west along the middle of the curve. The other two villages occupy the extremities of the semicircle; they are twelve and eighteen miles respectively from the most central village, and about twenty miles apart. The names of the villages are listed immediately following with a short note on the situation of each one. The native names are listed first; hereafter only these names will be used in referring to the villages. The alternative names are adaptations of the Masai names for the villages. They are in current use by the government, but as they are not liked by the Sonjo, and are not widely known in any case, it seems preferable to use native village names in writing about the tribe. The size of each village will be indicated by the approximate number of houses, the total for the tribe being estimated at 1,200.

1. KHERI, Digodigo Juu (*ca.* 180 houses).—

2. EBWE, Digodigo Chini (*ca.* 160 houses).—These two adjoining villages shared a common palisade for defence, but in every other way they are separate and independent villages. The Masai evidently regarded them as a single village to which

they gave the name Digodigo. When it was realized by government officials that they were separate villages, the Masai name was qualified with the Swahili word *Juu* (upper) in the case of Kheri and *Chini* (lower) for Ebwe. They are situated on the same escarpment, Kheri on the upper and Ebwe on the lower slope, separated by a hundred yards of precipitous hillside. Government headquarters—consisting of native court, dispensary, and primary school—are located near these twin villages. The only shop in Sonjo territory is also located near by. The villages themselves are affected by these external institutions in only slightly greater degree than other villages. More of their people use the dispensary, because of its convenient location, and a somewhat higher proportion go to school. In all essential respects they are typical Sonjo villages. In relation to the other villages, Kheri and Ebwe occupy a central position on the semicircle. My own camp was located about a quarter of a mile from Kheri and just a little farther from Ebwe.

3. SOYETU, Samunge (*ca.* 300 houses).—Located four miles south-west of Ebwe, this is the largest of the Sonjo villages, and near it is the site of the Lutheran mission station, consisting of a small church and a 'bush school'—i.e. a two-year primary school which does not necessarily satisfy government qualifications. In mythology, Soyetu is the scene of most of Khambageu's earthly activities; as a result it possesses many sacred places and shrines. The people of Soyetu have had more contact with the outside world than the other villages, with Kheri and Ebwe ranking next in this respect.

4. ROKHARI, Kisangero (*ca.* 120 houses).—This village, located four miles north-east of the twin villages, contains the principal temples and the headquarters of the priesthood and serves as a religious centre for the tribe. It is ultra-conservative in its attitude to the outside world. The elders have flatly refused permission for any kind of mission station or bush school in the village. Missionaries were not even allowed to enter the village to discuss the matter, according to a memorandum published by the Lutheran Church (Elikana *et al.* 1952). The temple precinct, occupying about a third of the village, is forbidden to everyone except people who are ritually pure; they may enter it to perform rites on special occasions. Although I

visited the village a number of times, I was always accompanied by several elders and my movements were restricted. Only once did I manage to view the temples. They seemed to be three connected structures, each resembling an ordinary house but twice the size.

5. KURA, Oldonyo Sambu (*ca.* 210 houses).—This village is twelve miles south-east of Kheri and Ebwe. Like Rokhari, it is built on a steeper and rougher slope than the other villages. It possesses a bush school operated by the mission, which, however, is located outside the village. The teacher stated that his work there is discouraging and his life intolerably lonesome. The most distinctive feature of Kura is its irrigation system, which differs in some respects from those of other villages; this will be described in chapter IV.

6. OROKHATA, Sale (*ca.* 230 houses).—This is the most remote of the Sonjo villages, being sixteen miles from its nearest neighbour, Soyetu. I made only one visit to Orokhata and thus have less information about it than the others. Because of its isolation and exposure to the Masai, its defensive palisade and fortified gates were more massive. The Lutheran Mission maintains a small chapel and a bush school just outside Orokhata.

Village layout

A village site is a rock-strewn hillside with much outcropping of bed rock. The natural steps in this rocky slope are utilized for house sites, and larger terraces are used as communal plazas. Most of the house sites have required some excavation in order to secure a level surface large enough for house building. Since excavation is only possible where the slope is not too steep or rocky, the spatial distribution of houses is somewhat irregular as determined by the topography. The aim was clearly to make the village as compact as possible within the limits of the nature and contours of the land. The house sites were made at considerable labour, and so they are regarded as valuable possessions of the clans to which they belong.

A Sonjo village is divided into territorial subdivisions called *nkaia*, which will hereinafter be referred to as 'wards'. A ward is occupied by the members of a single clan (*bukolo*), with a few other small groups attached in some cases. Clans, which are patrilineal descent groups, will be discussed in chapter

VIII. Since clans and wards are almost coterminous in membership, the two terms are interchangeable for some purposes; for
describing the physical arrangement of the village it is more
convenient to use 'ward'. The number of wards in a village
varies from three to six. Each ward has its own name. There is
sometimes a physical separation between wards—a cliff or
ravine or perhaps a main village path—but this separation is
not strictly necessary, and in some places the houses of one ward
interdigitate with those of another. The grouping of houses
within a ward depends as much on the contingencies of topography as on the interrelations of the occupants, and a stranger
is not usually able to deduce the nature and size of a family or
lineage group by observing the arrangement of the houses.
Nevertheless these groups do tend to build their houses in the
same quarter of a ward, and examples will be given in chapter
VIII.

Located somewhere near the centre of every Sonjo village is
a level cleared place large enough to accommodate several
hundred dancers. This is the village plaza, which is called the
keritone. It is the largest level area in the village and in most
places is situated in the upper part of the village commanding
a view of the country below. Its primary use is as a centre for
village festivals, and as these are all more or less religious in
nature, the plaza is treated as a sacred place. The floor is always
kept clear of rubbish and goat-droppings, even when no festival
is in prospect; the people are on good behaviour when they
rest there and do not laugh or talk loudly. One end of the plaza,
called the *khoseri*, contains a paddock-like enclosure of rough
logs in which the village council holds meetings. Behind that
is a small thatched structure constituting a sanctuary which is
very sacred and must never be entered by unauthorized persons. Some of the trees and stones in a plaza are also treated as
specially sacred. When one of these sacred trees starts ageing
its boughs are propped up with crutches to prevent them from
drooping. When some ritual is in progress the *khoseri* end of the
plaza is restricted to elders and warriors who are in a ritually
pure state and are wearing traditional skin garments. In
addition to the central village plaza there are plazas in each of
the wards, called *kaani*, which are replicas of the central plaza
but lacking a *khoseri* and usually considerably smaller. These

are used for the secular singing and dancing that takes place
in the village, and sometimes for special ritual. The use of
all plazas tends to be restricted to organized group activities.
For informal meeting places at which to lounge and talk the
men find shady nooks just outside the village.

Temples and shrines

Besides the main tribal temple at Rokhari, each village has
one or more temples. These are constructed like ordinary
houses and kept in repair by the community. Since they are
uninhabited they lack the smoke-blackened appearance of
houses and do not have the usual goat manure heaped in front
of their doors. The village temples are supervised by priests;
their use will be discussed in chapter vii. There are also a
number of other sacred places and objects in a Sonjo village.
Near the main gateway of every village, about fifty yards to
the right as you leave the village, stands a low shelter with a
conical thatched roof; it is about twenty feet in diameter and
has no walls, only a circle of posts. This is the guardhouse,
which in the old days was constantly manned by a company
of warriors. It is still kept in good repair and is now a sacred
structure used only for ritual purposes. Outsiders are not
allowed to approach near it, and I was told not to take a photograph of it. A survey of Soyetu—not necessarily complete—
revealed seven sacred places, not counting plazas, temples, or
the guardhouse. Two of these were of the nature of shrines and
were protected by low, thatched shelters. The others were
special rocks or trees, all of which had mythological associations and were used in special rites. There are still other sacred
places outside the villages.

Village fortifications

The most striking feature of a Sonjo village is undoubtedly
the picturesque gateway through which one passes in entering
the village. It is about ten feet wide and high enough for the
tallest man to walk through comfortably. The construction is
of heavy timbers: on each side of the passage a stout post made
from a forked tree is planted firmly. A thick beam is then laid
across the forks of the posts as a lintel. A second frame is built
about twelve feet inside the first and in line with it. A roof of

strong timbers is laid between the beams of the two frames; then a wall of horizontal railings is built above the outer gate frame as a parapet. A second post is planted behind each of the main gateposts, and the gate can be closed by piling logs across the opening so that their ends are held in the slot between the two posts. The purpose of the roof was to provide a platform for archers in time of attack. A few feet to the right of the main gate, as you approach it from the outside, is a small wicket gate, large enough for a man to crawl through with difficulty but easily accommodating goats. This was to provide entrance for stragglers and goats who remained outside after the gates had been closed; it could be easily guarded with a club or spear against enemies who might try to enter through it.

A palisade of timbers somewhat smaller than the gateposts extends ten yards or so from each side of the gate. Most of these timbers are made of forked trees or branches on which the limbs of the forks were left standing to a height of ten to twenty feet; the forks are neatly trimmed and pointed on the ends, and an annular mark is carved round the base. On some of the timbers second forks are left at the ends of the primary forks. A second gateway, similar to the outer one, was built about sixty yards inside the first. This served as a second line of defence in case the outer gate was breached. At Orokhata a third gateway was built inside the second; the full triple set of gateways still exists there.

The villages were formerly surrounded by dense thickets, pierced only by the gates. This has nearly all been cut for firewood; only a stretch of thicket extending from the main gateway for one or two hundred yards still exists, and this now constitutes a sacred grove. Judging from this remnant, the hedge must have been impenetrable to invaders. Various species of thorny shrubs and trees are growing as closely together as possible, and the mass is further strengthened by euphorbia trees whose rope-like branches interlace with the thorn bushes. The hedge appears to have been about seventy yards thick. Although protection against Masai raids is not required now, the gateways are still kept in good repair.

ABANDONED VILLAGE SITES

In Sonjo mythology there is mention of some villages that were once occupied but later abandoned. The sites of at least four of these abandoned villages are definitely known, of which I was only able to visit one—Tinaga. This site, about ten miles from Kheri, is laid out on a rocky hillside in typical Sonjo fashion. The village was located on a sizable stream which is said to flow the year round. The house sites are easily discernible, but no trace remains of houses or gateways. It is assumed that Tinaga, and the other abandoned villages as well, were older than the present villages, but there is no concrete evidence that this is true. A little systematic excavation at the site might bring to light some evidence for establishing a chronology, or at least for cultural comparisons. The government has become aware of the agricultural possibilities of the Tinaga site and is considering a plan for clearing the area and reopening it for settlement.

A second abandoned site is of a village called Mej, and is located between Kura and Lake Natron. It is said to have had a stone gateway of which one pillar still stands. The warriors of Mej are supposed to have been intrepid raiders who frequently stole Masai goats, until finally the Masai attacked the village in force and destroyed it.

Two other ruined villages whose sites are known are Khohani and Yasi. These are also said to have been overwhelmed by the Masai, but details of their histories were not known by my informants. Some of the present Sonjo claim to be descendants of the inhabitants of Khohani and Yasi; these are small groups living in wards which belong to regular clans, but not claiming relationship with these clans. A fifth village called Njem apparently had no survivors. The story is told that a German military force pitched camp there and carried out some punitive measures against the Masai. The Masai held the people of the village accountable for this, and when the Germans left they attacked and wiped out the village.

D

Chapter III

ECONOMIC BASIS OF SOCIETY

AGRICULTURE

THE agriculture year includes two complete crop cycles —one in the dry season and the other in the rainy season. As my field work lasted for just half a year, I was unable to observe all of both cycles and relied partly on the descriptions of informants. The two sets of agricultural operations are carried out on different kinds of land. The first kind is located in the flat bottom of the valley belonging to the village, and this is cultivated in the dry season entirely under irrigation. This land is distinguished by the name *hura*, and will hereinafter be referred to by that term. The soil of *hura* fields is heavy alluvial loam, black or dark red in colour. The whole valley is often flooded during the rainy season, which periodically renews the fertility of the soil so that crops can be planted on the same plots year after year. *Hura* cultivation starts in September, the first task being carried out by the men, who flood the fields to soften the ground and then pull up or dig up the stalks and large weeds from the previous year. This is not difficult work and is usually performed by a man working alone or with the help of his sons. Thereafter, a man's share of the work is limited to flooding the fields periodically with irrigation water.

The women then arrive on the scene with digging-sticks and first clear off and burn the trash which the men have left behind. Then the back-breaking work of loosening the soil begins. A seed bed is prepared by digging up the whole field to a depth of six or eight inches. The only implement is a digging-stick (*molo*, pl. *meleo*) about five feet long with a bevelled point. The digging-stick is used with a special technique which involves a rhythmic movement of the body akin to that of the prevailing dance technique. The stick is grasped by the hand about a foot from the point, the woman's body is flexed sharply at the hips, and she plunges the point into the ground. The loosened clod of earth is then thrown backwards between the legs with the free hand. The woman stands in loose earth and faces the unbroken soil as she works. Groups of from six to twenty women are usually seen working together for the initial cultivating of a field. They form a line which works from one end of the field to the other. When the first woman's fields are finished the whole group moves to the next woman's, and so on until all the fields are ploughed. This work is done during the heat of the day. While working in groups they always sing work songs, without which the work would be intolerably hard and tiresome. The rest of the agricultural work—planting, weeding, and harvesting—is done by each woman alone, or with the help of daughters or perhaps a daughter-in-law. This requires a period of field work almost every day. The daily routine of a housewife starts early in the morning with a trip to the stream for water, which may involve an hour's climb down the steep path and up again. The rest of the morning is spent working at home or resting or gossiping with other women. After an early noon meal with the family she goes to her fields, carrying a digging-stick and calabashes, and perhaps also an infant, if she has one with no older daughter to look after it. The empty calabashes are left at the main stream, as she crosses it, to await her return. When her afternoon's work is finished she stops at the stream to bathe and rest in the shade with other women, then she fills her calabashes and returns home to prepare the evening meal.

Sweet potatoes (*ngwazi*) are the principal crop grown on *hura* land, followed closely by pennisetum or bulrush millet (*bulo*) and several varieties of sorghum (*buheembe*). Beans and two or three kinds of cow peas are often grown interspersed in the fields of grain or sweet potatoes. These legumes are valued as much for their leaves, which are picked fresh and cooked as spinach, as for the pod seeds, which, however, are harvested when ripe and provide food rich in protein. Cassava is grown in small amounts at the instigation of the government agriculture department, but it is not liked as food.

In addition to his *hura* land, every man has a second set of fields, called *magare*, which are located on higher land sloping up from the valley. *Magare* soil is lighter and sandier than that of the *hura* land, but it is capable of producing abundant crops if it receives enough water. These fields are cultivated during the rainy season and the crops are watered by both rainfall and irrigation. Since the upper limit of the *magare* fields is considerably higher than the valley bottom, not as much irrigation water can be brought to them (see chapter iv, especially Fig. 1). Unlike *hura* land, *magare* land is only cultivated every second year and allowed to lie fallow on alternate years, so every man has two complete sets of these fields. In a year of good rainfall the *magare* land will produce crops without supplementary irrigation, but such years are rare in Sonjo memories. The division of labour in the cultivation of this land follows the same pattern that was described for *hura* fields, only the custom of co-operative work is reversed as regards men and women. In the *magare* fields the initial clearing is done by groups of from ten to twenty men, working in the dry soil and moving in rotation from one set of fields to the next. Women, on the other hand, cultivate their *magare* fields individually, each woman working with only the help of her daughters. As the soil is light and friable, the work of cultivating the fields with digging-sticks is easier than in the *hura* valley. Sorghum is the principal crop, with millet second in importance. Cow peas and pigeon peas are also grown. A type of bean known as *sonjo*, from which the tribe was given its name,[1] can only be grown on *magare* land, as it requires a light sandy soil.

The harvesting of *hura* crops starts with a first-fruits ceremony, which will be described in chapter vii, but no rites are performed at the *magare* harvest. The technique of harvesting grain crops is simple. The heads of grain are cut individually while they are still a little green (to minimize damage and loss from birds) and laid out on a bed of dry stalks to dry for a few days. The grain is stripped from the heads by hand and spread out on skins to dry further. Then it is winnowed and packed into leather bags to be carried home. In the houses the grain is stored in containers of whole goatskins, though nowadays

[1] Concerning the name, Wakefield (1870 : 317) writes: 'The name Sonjo is Kikwavi, and means "fiwi" (Kiswahili), a large species of bean. The Wakwavi sometimes buy beans (fiwi) from the Wasonjo.' The first Germans to arrive evidently borrowed the name from their Masai guides. It is now established in government usage and appears on all maps of the region. Therefore I decided to use the name Sonjo in preference to the native name Batemi.

cow-skin storage containers are coming into use. In a normal year the grain crop from *magare* fields should last about six months, or until the *hura* crop is harvested. When the *magare* crop falls short of this amount, the deficiency must be made good with early sweet potatoes, of which several crops can be grown in a season if necessary.

LIVESTOCK

Goats and sheep are raised in the ratio of about six goats to one sheep. I shall not hereafter distinguish between them, as they are equivalent in value, except for fat-tailed sheep which are worth two goats or ordinary sheep. A livestock census in progress during my stay was just completed at the village of Soyetu before I left. Preliminary returns revealed a total of 8,543 goats divided among 158 owners—an average of about 54 goats for an owner. Like most African stock raisers, the Sonjo dislike telling the number of animals that they own. According to estimates made by neighbours in the same village, the numbers of animals owned by individuals varies from ten to fifteen to over a thousand. It is the usual practice for a man to divide his goats into two herds, one (consisting of young animals and females in milk) being kept in the village and the other sent to a camp several miles away from the village. The home herd is kept in the house at night and is herded in and near the village by young boys. The small kids and lambs are kept in a pen and fed on green leaves. The young men of a village vie with one another in climbing the tallest trees to cut leaves, and occasionally fall and injure themselves. The female animals are milked by housewives morning and night. The milk is used as food and also churned into butter. The urine of goats is believed to be beneficial in a house by reducing the vermin.

The main herds are kept at permanent camps located out on the plain at distances of from three to eight miles from the cultivated area. From these camps the goats are taken out to graze and browse during the day, and at night they are brought into special shelters. The latter are about the same size as a village house, but with walls that are strongly reinforced with timbers so that leopards, which infest the area, cannot easily break in. A camp may contain only a single shelter or a cluster of three or four. They are in charge of uninitiated boys—two boys to a shelter. In order to make the herds more manageable, all male animals are castrated when they reach full size at about six months. The technique is to strangulate the scrotum with a bow string and then pound the testicles with an elongated stone which is specially shaped and smoothed for this purpose. Breeding is thus limited to young males before their castration or to those with undescended testes, of which the natives say there is a high incidence. Goats are marked for identification in two ways: by clipping the ears with distinctive notches and branding the neck or face with a hot iron. Every clan has its own set of marks applied to all goats belonging to the members of the clan. Individual owners are supposed to be able to recognize their own goats by sight and so it is not necessary to brand them with individual marks. These customs do not mean that there is anything like joint ownership of goats by a whole clan—ownership is strictly individual—and there is really no adequate explanation for the use of a clan mark unless it is a survival from former times. The social implications of this custom will be considered again in discussing village political organization. The goat camps belonging to a single clan tend to be grouped in the same part of the pasture, and by having the goats of those camps marked with the same brand the herd boys find it easier to keep their goats from mixing with other herds, but this hardly explains the custom adequately.

Goats are valued economically for their milk, hides, and meat, and as a standard unit of trade to barter for other goods such as grain or honey. They are used for ritual sacrifices, and exchanged for rights to irrigation water. The bride-price—which is comparatively high among the Sonjo—is also comprised of goats. The details of these exchanges will be discussed in later chapters.

HONEY

The Sonjo are skilful in attracting wild bees to their hives, and honey plays an important part in their economy. The hives (*moringa*, pl. *meringa*) are carved from carefully selected hardwood logs and are said to last as long as fifty years. The making of a hive involves hard work and they are regarded as valuable property. As they are very heavy to carry they are usually put in trees near the place of manufacture. Hives are placed in the forks of large trees, usually at a considerable height from the ground. This is a delicate engineering feat requiring the co-operation of several men. First the hive is laid in a cradle of heavy sticks and the whole bundle is tied with leather thongs. Then a stout leather strap is passed over a limb which is above the fork to be used, and one end of the strap is attached to the hive. The men on the ground hoist the hive up by pulling on the loose end of the strap, while another man climbs the tree and eases the hive into position in the tree fork, resting on its cradle of sticks.

Some elders have as many as a hundred hives scattered about the country, and most men have at least twenty. The men are constantly on the lookout for trees which appear to be fav-ourable for placing hives. When such a tree is located the finder cuts a hooked stick and hangs it on the exact fork where he plans to place his hive. As long as his stick hangs there he has a right to that location, though other hives can be placed in different forks of the same tree—as many as eight were counted in large trees. The crop of honey is said to vary from year to year according to weather and other factors affecting bees. A normal expectation is to find that six hives have been occupied by bees in a year. This would yield about thirty gallons of honey altogether. In gathering the honey, the bees are smoked out; then a man climbs the tree with a leather bag attached to a long strap. He scoops the honey into the bag and lowers it by the strap to a helper on the ground. It is dangerous work and nearly always involves getting stung by bees. Only the young men undertake to do it. The honey itself, however, all goes to the owner who is usually an older man.

Honey is so highly valued because it is made into a honey beer or hydromel which is the only alcoholic beverage known to the Sonjo. The same word is used to designate either 'honey' or 'beer'—*bukhoma*. A small portion is set aside for the women and children to be eaten as a sweet or made into an unfer-mented drink, but the bulk of it is used for beer. Beer drinking is an exclusive prerogative of elders—the older a man is the more he can drink with propriety—and the young men of the

warrior class are strictly forbidden to drink. Beer is drunk informally for pleasure and also ritually at religious celebrations;
it is used for libations at rites for which the slaughter of a goat
is not required. It is a symbol of hospitality and should be
produced when an elder is visited by his age-mates from different villages. Honey has a stable market value, and a standard
jar containing three to four gallons of honey is exchanged for
one goat. Through the exchange system a wealthy man (as
judged by goats) is able to augment his supply of beer, and a
poor man who has luck with his hives is able to acquire goats
and build up his herd. Honey is commonly used by the lower
economic class in obtaining secondary rights to irrigation water,
as will be explained in the next chapter.

DWELLINGS AND GARMENTS

The necessary materials for house building are readily available
in the nearby forests and fields, but the construction requires
the co-operation of a number of men. It is customary for a man
to build his first house at the time of his first marriage. His
father-in-law is expected to furnish half the material, and the
other men of his ward help with the building, which takes two
or three days. First a circle of forked posts are planted in the
ground, then a ring of beams are laid over the forks. Four
longer poles, also forked, are planted in the middle of the house
and short beams are laid over their forks. After that a large
number of long withes are applied to this rough frame; the butt
ends are planted in the ground, the withes are bent over the
beams, and their small ends are tied together at the apex of
the house. After the doorway has been fashioned with a special
frame, the women take over and thatch the house to the ground.
When thatched with fresh grass the house resembles a dome-
shaped haystack if viewed from the rear. A proper Sonjo door
is made of a single hewed plank, which involves a great deal
of labour and is said to last for several generations. If a young
house-builder is not in a position to inherit a plank door, he
usually makes do with a rough wicker-work door until such
time as he is able to obtain a proper door. A polygynist must
provide a separate house for each of his wives, but the ultimate
ownership of these houses remains with the husband. Thus a

divorced wife has no claim on her house, and when the husband remarries he may install his new wife in the same house.

The Sonjo traditionally clothed themselves entirely in skins, and this is still largely true today. The basic garment for both sexes is a large rectangle of goat skins which is worn as a cloak. Most adults have several of these cloaks, the tattered ones being used for everyday wear and the newer ones for dress occasions. The goat skins to be used for cloaks are cleaned and stretched in the sun to dry. Then the hair is scraped off with a hafted iron implement which is also used unhafted as a razor —a spatula-shaped blade sharpened on the broad end. The skins are trimmed and sewed together, using goat sinew for thread and an iron awl to pierce holes in the skin. As the skins are not softened by any special treatment they are stiff when new, but gradually become softer with use and conform some- what to the curve of the shoulders. Women's cloaks are usually decorated along the edge with large beads spaced six to ten inches apart. Sometimes small beads are sewed on a garment to form a simple design. This cloak is all that a man normally wears, but women wear small leather skirts or girdles under- neath. The latter are of two kinds which differ according to whether a woman has borne a child or not. Nulliparous women wear a band of leather which has been slit vertically into nar- row thongs, leaving a beaded belt round the hips; in appearance it resembles a short grass skirt. Women with children wear a similar girdle but unslit, that is, a solid band of leather, from ten to fifteen inches wide, round the hips. These garments are pleated in the back to allow ample leg movement. Both kinds are made of goat skins which are treated with fat to make them soft and pliable. They are worn very low so that the top of the skirt just covers the pubic area in front, and they are held in place by an adjustable thong tied round the top.

The wearing of clothing is regulated by definite rules of modesty. The women wear only their girdles when working in the house or at the fields. There is no embarrassment if other men of the village see them thus uncloaked, except for their fathers or adult brothers, but at all other places a woman is expected to be decently covered by a cloak. Small girls from the time they are first able to walk wear a miniature version of the maidens' girdle with a fringe only two or three inches long.

Young boys, though, are allowed to run naked until they are old enough to herd goats; then they wear a goat skin fastened over one shoulder, but they are still careless about exposing their bodies. Initiated boys must follow strict rules requiring them to be decently clothed in front of other people in the village; an exception is made at the harvest festival, when they dance virtually naked. For other dress occasions they wear a special skirt made of soft, chamois-like goat skin. Young elders are quite careful about modesty in their dress, but older ones are often careless, almost as if deliberately, and will sometimes get up from a seat, even in a public place, and open their cloaks to adjust them, leaving their bodies momentarily stark naked.

SMITHS AND POTTERS

The name Moturi is used to designate either a smith or a member of the Waturi clan, whose men are the smiths and whose women the potters of the tribe. These people formerly lived at every village, but the availability of imported iron goods in recent times has so reduced their volume of work that they are now found only in the villages of Kheri and Ebwe. The clan now comprises about thirty males who are supposed to be divided into two lineages which intermarry. The Waturi regard themselves as related to the Masai smiths (called *Il-kunono* by the Masai) and may have originated from them. The chief production of the smiths at present is arrow points (*vilango*), which are made from coarse trade wire, razors (*ndugenda*), knives (*ndakhuyu*), and adze blades (*khonosili*). They formerly made the Sonjo sword (*lohyo*) which is similar to the *sime* of the Masai. Now, however, unfinished blanks for sword blades, made of tempered steel and imported from Germany, can be bought at Arusha cheaply and are much preferred to the native product. The warriors bring these blanks to the smiths, who finish and sharpen the blades and fit them with handles. Axes and machetes were traditionally made by the local smiths, but are now mostly purchased at the shop.

A blacksmith's bellows consists of two pouches made of whole goat skins and joined at the narrow ends to a bifurcated wooden tube which fits into a clay funnel leading to the charcoal forge. The broad open end of each pouch is attached to two parallel strips of wood which are grasped by the hand to open and close the pouch. By alternately filling each bag with air, closing it, and slowly collapsing it, a continuous stream of air is fed into the fire. The anvil is simply a smooth rock. The working tools include hammers of different sizes and an assortment of hinged tongs, all made by the blacksmith himself. The raw iron, except for the commercial wire, is obtained from Masai smiths and consists mostly of broken spears.

The women of the Waturi clan make all the pottery for the Sonjo—cooking pots, jars for storing water, and plates. The clay is mined in special caves and excavations which are strictly taboo for other people. It is dried in the sun, powdered, mixed with water and sand, and moulded by hand in the shape of the required vessel; this is dried in the sun and then fired in a pit, using dried goat dung for fuel. Finished pottery is bartered for standard measures of grain. Waturi are not permitted to own fields or do any cultivating, so they are obliged to sell pottery in order to obtain vegetable food. The men of the clan, however, are allowed to keep goats.

HANDICRAFTS

Apart from the smiths and potters there are no full-time specialists among the Sonjo, and it is not uncommon for a naturally skilled man to make all his non-metal implements himself, but there is a certain amount of informal specialization in the making of precision items such as bows and arrow shafts. A good woodworker possesses the knowledge for choosing the right kind of wood for various implements and for seasoning it properly as well as skill in carving it. Most of the leather working is done by the women. Ordinary cloaks can be made by any woman, but girdles require more skill, and there is some specialization in their manufacture. The Sonjo have no basketry of any kind; instead they make a variety of leather pouches and bags for carrying and storing goods. Leather straps are used in place of ropes, mainly for the work of hoisting beehives and gathering honey. Other items of leather are quivers, scabbards, and knife sheathes. Bow strings are made from the fascia of a goat's back muscles. Certain old men specialize in this work and sit all day in the shade fashioning strings from the wet fibres. The Sonjo keep their bows strung at all times so that the string has be to renewed at intervals.

Sonjo women grind their grain by the simple saddle-quern technique which is common in other tribes in the region. The equipment consists of a flat rectangular lower stone, over which the woman kneels astride, and a small upper stone which is pushed backwards and forwards to grind the grain. Material for making grindstones is plentiful at all the villages. Smaller grindstones or mortars are used for grinding snuff and pigments used in skin paints—red ochre and white clays.

Calabashes are used for carrying liquids, though water is usually stored in clay jars. Locally grown calabashes are round or pear-shaped. Those used for beer drinking have a bulbous neck partially separated from the body of the gourd by a constriction. They are often highly polished and are wound round the neck with a leather thong, leaving a loop for carrying by the hand. Bowls for mixing food and feeding infants are also made from local gourds. The other kind of gourd, elongated in the shape of a cucumber, is used in carrying water from the stream and milk from the goat camp. These are grown at temporary settlements on the shore of Lake Natron. The Masai also use these long slender gourds and often buy them from the Sonjo.

MONEY ECONOMY

Although I have described the Sonjo economy as if it still operated entirely by barter, a certain amount of money now enters the tribe as wages paid to the young men who work as migrant labourers. This money is used for buying trade goods and paying taxes. Money, however, is seldom involved in exchange transactions within the tribe. Bride-price is always paid in livestock and money cannot be used as a substitute. Fees for the use of irrigation water are normally paid in goods—usually goats, honey, or grain—though there is no strict rule against the use of money for this purpose.

Chapter IV

THE IRRIGATION SYSTEM

IN this chapter the irrigation system of the village of Kheri will be described in some detail, with descriptions of the sources of irrigation water, the network of furrows and ditches, the operation of the system, and the control and regulation of water. The general pattern of the irrigation system as described for Kheri also exists, with only minor variations, at two of the other villages—Ebwe and Soyetu—whose irrigation systems were inspected during the course of the field study. At each of these villages the water supply is derived from a small stream coming down from the hills and considerably augmented in the vicinity of the villages with the water from springs. The combined water from these sources enters the cultivated area as a large channel, and is divided into branch furrows which ramify through the fields, bringing water to every plot. Except in years of unusual rainfall, the water is completely used up for irrigation during the dry months and is therefore regarded as a scarce commodity which is carefully conserved and divided among users according to definite rules.

As explained in the last chapter, two different kinds of fields are cultivated at these villages. The flat alluvial land in the valley floors, distinguished by the term *hura*, is cultivated during the dry season entirely by irrigation. Crops are planted here every year on the same plots, as the soil does not seem to require fallow periods to maintain its fertility. This *hura* land is entirely taken up by individual owners, although every plot is not cultivated every year, and according to all informants it has been under cultivation for several generations in the past. The other kind of field, called *magare*, is located on the sloping land which rises gently from the valley floors. These fields are tilled during the rainy season and normally require both rainfall and irrigation to provide adequate moisture for crops, though in wet years supplementary irrigation may not be required. The amount of *magare* land that can be brought under cultivation at any one time is limited by the amount of water available for irrigating it. Therefore, tenure of these fields involves rights to irrigation water, for without water the plots would be worthless.

My information about irrigation at the other three villages is incomplete. On my one visit to Orokhata I was not able to make any field observations of the irrigation system; therefore the descriptions and analyses in this chapter will not necessarily apply to that village. Cursory surveys at Rokhari and Kura revealed some important differences between their irrigation systems and the system at Kheri. At Rokhari a spring located very near the village supplies water for irrigating a comparatively small area. This spring, though, has a ritual significance for the whole tribe that is disproportionate to its size or economic importance. The main area of cultivation is in a valley watered by a perennial stream. Informants stated that the annual schedule of agriculture events at Rokhari—irrigation, planting, harvesting, and the like—is somewhat different from the schedule followed at Kheri.

The hydraulic situation at Kura is unique among Sonjo villages in that water is plentiful but land is scarce. There, all the arable land is located in the floor of a single valley with steeply sloping sides to which irrigation water cannot be brought. A river flowing through the valley provides an abundance of water for irrigation, even during the dry months of the year. Most of the irrigable land is now in use, and thus there is little possibility of expanding the agriculture of the village with traditional hydraulic techniques. On the other hand, to compensate for the limitation of land, two crops a year are said to be raised on the same fields at Kura, but detailed information on this agricultural cycle is lacking. The villages of Orokhata, Rokhari, and Kura all have village councils which appear to be constituted in much the same way as the Kheri council and to have similar control over irrigation water.

We turn now to a more detailed description of the Sonjo irrigation system as found at Kheri. The schematic diagram in Figure 1 should be referred to in reading the following account.

SOURCES OF IRRIGATION WATER

The valley cultivated by the people of Kheri narrows at its northern end to a steep defile through which a stream flows into the valley. The course of the stream follows close to the base of the escarpment which forms the western wall of the valley and on the slopes of which the twin villages of Kheri and

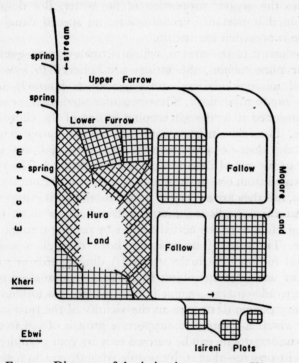

FIG. I.   Diagram of the irrigation system at Kheri

Ebwe are located. It is joined by the water from three springs rising from a spring line near the bottom of the escarpment. The stream flows to the valley from the general direction of the Loliondo highlands in the north. Its ultimate source seems to be of no special interest to the villagers. It is not one of the major streams flowing from the highlands and appears to drain a comparatively small area. According to my own estimate, made in mid dry season, the stream supplies about a quarter

of the total water supply. On the other hand, during the rainy
season, when water for irrigation is not required, the stream
increases greatly in flow and frequently inundates the whole
valley bottom. These periodic floods undoubtedly maintain the
fertility of the valley soil by depositing alluvium, thus making
it possible to plant crops year after year on the same plots.
During the period when *magare* crops are irrigated the stream
supplies the greater proportion of the water. But despite its
undoubted importance economically, no special ritual significance is accorded the stream.

In contrast to the stream, which is treated as an essentially
secular phenomenon, the springs are believed to have been
created miraculously and are regarded as intensely sacred.
According to mythology, Khambageu created each spring and
then assigned it to the safekeeping of one of the clans of the
village. The relation between a clan and its spring is purely
ritual and does not give the members of the clan any special
rights to the use of the spring water in irrigation. The springs
are located from one to two hundred yards away from the main
stream, but they are so hedged in by taboos that it is impossible,
without causing offence, for an outsider to get more than a
fleeting glimpse of the actual springs by peering through dense
foliage. The water from a spring flows through a well-kept
channel to enter the main stream. A dozen yards or so back
from the stream, some object by the spring channel—a rock or
a tree trunk—marks a point beyond which it is forbidden for
ordinary people to trespass in the vicinity of the springs. This
area, which is damp and supports a growth of tall trees and
dense undergrowth, can be entered only by young children and
very old people—that is, by people who are not in a sexually
active period of life. This injunction is very strictly observed,
and no exception would be considered in my own case when I
requested permission to examine the springs more closely.
Ordinary rites in connexion with the spring are enacted just
outside this forbidden area.

A few plots at the narrow head of the valley, amounting to
only five or six acres, are irrigated with water from the stream
alone above the point where the first spring joins it, but the
bulk of the land is irrigated with a mixture of stream and spring
water. The stream water used on those upper plots is controlled

by the village council in the same way as the mixed water lower down. One of the two main irrigation furrows branches off from the stream below the first spring. This is used just after the rains finish to conduct water to the *magare* fields. The second furrow leaves the stream below the second spring and is the principal channel for irrigating the *hura* fields. The water from the third spring is also used on the *hura* fields.

There is some seasonal variation in the flow of water from the springs, according to Sonjo informants, but it is nothing like the extreme fluctuations of the stream. By comparison, the springs seem to supply a stable and dependable flow which is not obviously controlled by rainfall or other climatic factors. Thus they tend to be viewed as autonomous phenomena, essentially different in their nature from streams resulting from ordinary surface drainage, a view which is reinforced by the mythological belief in their supernatural origin.

The abundance of a harvest in an average year is probably as much dependent on direct rainfall as on irrigation. In a year of very low or badly timed rainfall there may be a total loss of crop on *magare* land and a decreased *hura* crop. But no matter how little the rainfall, the springs always supply enough water to ensure that some crop is harvested from the *hura* fields —at least enough to avert outright famine. The attitudes towards these two sources of moisture are quite different. Rainfall is regarded as part of the external natural environment, unpredictable and uncontrollable. Unlike most of the cultivating tribes in semi-arid regions of Africa, (the Sonjo do not attempt to manipulate rainfall by direct magic in order to allay their anxiety.) There is no separate cult of rainmaking. Instead, the element of supernatural rainmaking is merged with the dominant religious cult of the tribe. Anxiety as to the danger of drought is made tolerable through faith in Khambageu, prayer, and general religious ritual. The orthodox belief asserts that as long as good relations exist between Khambageu and the people God will ensure adequate rainfall. These relations are maintained by the right conduct of the people, both ritual and moral, by subjective thoughts and feelings as well as by overt behaviour. If rain or other natural benefits are withheld, it is believed that basic rules of conduct have been violated, angering God, even though the particular transgressions may

E

not be publicly known. Rain is specifically requested as a
blessing in all public prayers, which also routinely include re-
quests for health and fecundity of people, flocks, and crops. It
is significant that the formal prayer for rain is stated in a hydraulic metaphor—'Open the sluices of Belwa.' Irrigation is a
central them in Sonjo religion as well as in agriculture. In the
imagery of the prayer, rainfall is related to this theme by being
imagined as the overflow from a celestial irrigation system.)

The attitude towards the springs is conservative and ritualistic. The springs do not fluctuate unpredictably and have never
been known to fail, but if fluctuation or failure should occur
the results would be more catastrophic than in the case of
drought. They are conceived of as in a different category from
unpredictable blessings such as rain or health. Moreover, owing
to their supernatural origin they are thought of as specifically
sacred objects, not just natural phenomena. Therefore the
basic policy in regard to springs is directed at maintaining the
unchanging state of affairs that has prevailed in the past. Their
sacredness is acknowledged by meticulously performing the
traditional ritual concerning springs. They are treated as sanc-
tuaries and may not be approached by ordinary people who are
involved in sexual activities and the passions of everyday life,
which are considered to be antithetical to the sacred atmosphere
of objects and ritual dedicated to Khambageu. Thus they are
effectively insulated against contact with the profane world,
which might contaminate and weaken their sanctity and
introduce disastrous change.

FURROWS AND SLUICES

Owing to the circumstances that the sources of water are close
to the cultivated fields and that the land is relatively flat, no
very difficult works of hydraulic engineering were required in
constructing the irrigation systems at any of the villages.[1] At
Kheri the two main sluices for controlling the water are located
just below the first and second springs respectively. The few
plots above the first spring are irrigated through small ditches
leading directly off the main stream. At the points where the

---

[1] Widtsoe (1920 : 189–215, 419–44) discusses the methods and problems of constructing and maintaining irrigation channels under various conditions.

main furrows fork off, sluices have been built on each limb of
the fork. These are simply earth dams reinforced with revet-
ments of small timbers. By manipulating the sluices the water
may be shunted entirely into one of the channels, or it may be
divided so as to flow concurrently through several of them.
The sluices are opened by merely removing enough earth from
the dam to allow the desired flow of water. The earth is piled
on the bank and is later replaced in the dam when it is time
to shut off the water through that channel.

At each of these main bifurcations the branch on the right
(or west) is a continuation of the original stream bed. This
channel flows southwards from the second spring for about a
mile, being joined by the third spring half way down; it then
turns east, following the margin of the *hura* land in its whole
course. When no water is needed for irrigation (i.e. during
rains) all the water is directed through this channel to by-pass
the cultivated area. The upper main furrow, which carries
water to the *magare* fields, will be discussed later. The second
main furrow branches off from the main stream at an angle
and curves round the eastern edge of the *hura* fields, regaining
the main stream at the lower end of the valley. This furrow
feeds water to about three-fourths of the *hura* area, and thus
in the dry season, when *hura* plots are tilled, it carries three-
fourths of the total water supply. The other fourth is supplied
by the third spring.

From this large furrow and from the stream a number of
smaller channels branch off into the cultivated area; these in
turn subdivide into still smaller channels which will be found
to coincide with the boundaries of individual plots. The plots
are small and most of them are roughly rectangular in shape,
so that their boundaries describe a reticular network spread
evenly over the whole area. Every line in the network is a
potential irrigation channel. Water is brought where it is
needed by opening or closing the proper sluices, located at the
corners of plots, and thus connecting up a direct channel
through which water can be made to flow to any designated
plot. This picture is slightly oversimplified because the plots
tend to be grouped in blocks of a dozen or so, whose boundaries
are often marked by larger channels which may be used in
preference to the inter-plot channels if water is to by-pass the

whole block. This system can be best visualized as a fine network of small channels reinforced by a superimposed coarser network of larger channels. The high degree of uniformity of this network of channels is due to the even gradient of the valley bottom from north to south and (more gradual) from east to west. When the irrigation system is in operation it is normally expected that the water will be wholly consumed at the plots. However, the network of channels is tilted towards the lower end of the valley, so that if there is an excess of moisture—as happened during my visit, for example, following an unexpected rain—it drains in that general direction, ultimately to rejoin the main stream in its exit from the valley. When it does rain irrigation water is normally not wanted for a few days; then the sluices are closed and the water is shunted round the valley through the main stream bed till needed again.

The first furrow leaves the stream relatively high in its course, and thus it cannot carry water from the second and third springs. This is owing to the necessity of starting the furrow at the highest possible elevation in order that water can be delivered at a high enough level up on the sloping *magare* to irrigate a sufficiently large area. In following a level course over uneven ground at a relatively high elevation at the foot of a bluff, this furrow winds more than the other main furrow and requires deeper cuts and more massive dikes in its construction. It terminates at the upper boundary of the *magare* fields; there it subdivides into branches leading into the several blocks of plots. The *magare* plots are more regular in their rectangular shape and more uniform in size than the *hura* plots, but like the latter the plots are bounded by ditches through which irrigation water is directed to where it is needed. *Magare* land is tilled every second year and left fallow on alternate years, so there are two complete sets of fields. The *magare* furrow is opened when the annual rains appear to be finished and the ground starts to dry out. It is kept open till the grain has ripened, and is then closed off to remain idle for the rest of the year.

There is still a third type of crop land, which is cultivated much like the *hura* plots, but which is different enough to be distinguished by a special term—*isireni*. This consists of several natural terraces of land downstream from the *hura* valley. It

I*a*. Framework of a house

I*b*. Woman cultivating with a digging-stick

measures about thirty acres altogether. The *isireni* irrigation system is more complicated than the *hura* system. Because of the different elevations of these terraces it is necessary in several places to use aqueducts made of hollowed logs for bridging furrows in order to bring water to awkwardly located plots. *Hura* plots are given priority for the use of water, so when water is scarce there may not be enough left over to irrigate the *isireni* land. For that reason the latter are not as highly valued, and owners do not rely entirely on *isireni* plots but must also possess *hura* and *magare* plots. The planting of these plots is done as early as possible in the hope that the crops will have reached maturity before irrigation water becomes scarce. Cassava, a recently introduced crop[1] which requires little or no irrigation, seems to thrive on *isireni* land, and an increasing proportion of the area is being planted in cassava.

From the *isireni* terraces the stream bed descends about a mile to the main watercourse, which is dry most of the year but becomes a raging torrent in heavy rains. A few small plots are laid out along the stream, but as so little water comes down from the cultivated areas above it is hardly considered worth while to plant crops here because of the danger of losing one's seed through drought. From time to time optimistic Sonjo are said to plant crops on land to which irrigation water cannot be brought, depending on rainfall alone, but nobody attempted this in the year of my field work.

CONSTRUCTION AND MAINTENANCE OF CHANNELS

The irrigation system as it now exists is believed to have been first laid out and built at the time the village was founded, as told in myth. Thereafter it was only necessary for the people to keep the system in good repair. Every year when the rains have finished and flood waters subsided the elders of the village council set a time for repairing the damage to furrows done by the rains and call out all the able-bodied men of the village to do this work. (Only the smiths are exempted: they are not

[1] Cassava was introduced by the agriculture department as a form of famine insurance, and by an administrative order every tax-payer is required to plant a quarter of an acre of his land in cassava. This order is not yet being strictly enforced, the people being allowed a few years to become accustomed to tilling the new crop.

allowed to cultivate or have anything to do with the irrigation system.) Channels which have silted up must be cleaned out and dikes rebuilt where they have washed away. Nowadays this work only takes about three days, but formerly it was a longer task. The difference lies in the implements which were used formerly and at present: traditionally the digging-stick was the only tool available for this work; now, however, many of the men possess iron hoes, which are much more efficient tools for digging and moving earth. The adoption of hoes is said to be quite recent—within the last six years.

The upper furrow leading to the *magare* fields requires most of the repair work. In its course along the foot of a bluff this furrow traverses a series of small ridges with hollows between them. The cuts through the ridges are six feet or more deep, while in the low places the channel is built up with dikes. The lower furrow follows more level ground and does not require such substantial dikes or deep cuts. The main stream bed itself is diked through most of its length; this is also repaired at the time of the annual corvée. The whole village is not called out again during the year unless an unexpected rain storm causes serious washouts which need repairing. The tasks of clearing the channels of local obstructions and making minor routine repairs are done by voluntary workers. Men who are due to receive irrigation water on a certain day examine and repair the channels to ensure that the full flow of water reaches their plots.

The smaller ditches forming the boundaries between plots are maintained jointly by the owners of the adjoining plots. There is no incentive for a man to shirk his share of this work, because in that case the ditch, and therefore the boundary, would tend to drift in his direction, decreasing the size of his plot. There is a temptation to work on these ditches in such a way that they gradually shift towards a neighbour's plot. In most plots the boundaries are marked by corner stones, but these too can be gradually shifted. Thus if an owner does not attend vigilantly to his boundary ditches he is liable to find his plot progressively shrinking to the enlargement of his neighbours' plots. To move a corner stone or boundary ditch is a serious offence carrying a heavy fine; but as there are few permanent landmarks in the alluvial soil of the valley it is difficult to detect this form of land

II*a*. A section of the village of Ebwe

II*b*. Wooden aqueduct crossing a lower
irrigation ditch

stealing if it is done little by little over a period of time. Minor disputes over boundary ditches frequently arise, but are usually settled informally between the owners and rarely result in a charge before the village council.

Let us now imagine that we are walking through the *hura* fields about noon on some day during the dry season observing the irrigation system in operation. We go to an area where six or eight men are standing about, some of them perhaps working in the ditches with digging-sticks. Some of the plots in the area will have water standing in them and others will be wet from recent flooding. Noon is the normal time for the morning irrigation period to end and for the afternoon period to start. Therefore the owners of the wet fields will be finishing their irrigation and blocking up the channels to cut off the water flowing into their plots. Other men will be manipulating sluices and clearing a channel to a new group of plots which are to be irrigated during the afternoon. An area which is irrigated in one period includes as many as ten or more plots which may be owned by two or three different men. These plots are usually located fairly close together, though not necessarily adjacent to one another. It is planned this way for the most efficient use of the water; thus there will be less waste than if the water were dispersed to different corners of the valley during a single morning or afternoon.

If we stay the whole afternoon observing we shall note that one man, who exercises the most authority, soaks his own plots thoroughly first. When his needs are satisfied the water is diverted in turn to the fields of his companions, who may not find time to soak their fields as thoroughly as they might wish before the period comes to an end with sundown. The first man has primary rights to the water for the afternoon period. He stands in a position of patron to the other men (or perhaps only one man) and allows them to use the water that is left over when his own needs are satisfied. Very likely in the course of the afternoon the area will be visited by several other men whom we recognize as members of the village council. They may offer advice or criticism or merely observe the operations of irrigation. One of the duties of the village council is to plan and direct the whole system of irrigation with a view to utilizing the water with maximum efficiency. The members use a good deal of their time observing and discussing the system. In the next section of this chapter we shall define the different categories into which the men of the village are grouped with respect to irrigation rights.

CONTROL AND DIVISION OF WATER

The ultimate control of irrigation water is in the hands of a council of seventeen village elders who hold their positions as members by hereditary right. These council members are called *wenamiji*[1] (sing. *mwenamiji*)—and will hereinafter be referred to by that term. The rest of the people of the village are grouped into several categories as regards their rights to the use of water. Before analysing these rights it must be explained that for purposes of irrigation the twenty-four-hour day is divided into four periods of roughly six hours each. Primary rights for water are assigned to an individual for a full six-hour period. When water is plentiful two or more men may be assigned irrigation periods concurrently for the same period. In fact, early in the dry season, when the furrows are full and little water is used, the irrigation system requires little management. But as the dry season advances and water becomes scarce the whole water supply is allotted to individuals in successive six-hour periods. The present discussion will presuppose conditions of water scarcity, for that is when the legal and economic principles governing the irrigation system come fully into operation. The analysis will refer specifically to the irrigation of *hura* fields, though the same principles apply *mutatis mutandis* to *magare* irrigation.

An irrigation cycle, during which all plots are supposed to be soaked once, lasts about fourteen days. In starting a cycle, the *wenamiji* assign themselves the first periods; this takes about four days. Next in order of priority comes a group of eighteen men called 'minor' *wenamiji* (*wenamiji barirage*) who also hold hereditary rights. In terms of individual water rights these men are equal to the *wenamiji* proper, but they have no control over the irrigation system as a whole and have no special powers in village government. The qualifying term 'minor' must not be

[1] Derived from *wana* ('children', or, in a more general sense, 'people of') and *miji* ('village'). The word now carries the special import of 'council member'.

understood to imply that these men are necessarily younger than the *wenamiji*, or that they have expectations of later succeeding to the position of *wenamiji* proper; they constitute an entirely separate group. The fact that the special term *wenamiji* is applied to both groups suggests that they might have had a common origin in the past, with the minor *wenamiji* perhaps developing as an offshoot of the original village council. However, I have no direct evidence supporting this conjecture.

After that the irrigation periods are assigned to a group of elders called *wakiama* (sing. *mokiama*), numbering from twenty to twenty-five, who have no hereditary or permanent water rights, but obtain temporary rights, through paying tribute to the *wenamiji*. The *wakiama*[1] represent substantial families of the village who lack inherited positions of privilege in regard to water, but who are able to pay for these privileges with goats. Individuals of this group are assigned irrigation rights for only short periods of time—month by month—and the number of *wakiama* fluctuates from time to time. The maximum number is limited by the need to keep the length of the cycle down to about fourteen days. *Hura* crops normally require irrigation every fourteen days and sometimes oftener; therefore the sum of the assigned periods is not permitted to exceed the optimum length for the whole cycle.

The above three categories—*wenamiji*, minor *wenamiji*, and *wakiama*—account for less than half of the men in the village who require irrigation water. The rest, who will be referred to as 'clients'[2] in the context of irrigation, have no primary rights but must apply for secondary water rights to individuals with primary rights who have been assigned regular periods in the irrigation schedule. An individual of the privileged categories seldom requires all the water for the six hours to which he is

[1] The root of this term (*kiama*) is a word in the Kikuyu language, and the same word or close cognates are found in a number of other Bantu languages. It has the general meaning of 'council of elders' (Middleton 1953 : 35–7). If we assume that the Sonjo term originally carried the general Bantu meaning, this might suggest that with the development of the irrigation system the men controlling irrigation water, the *wenamiji*, usurped the powers and functions of an original council of *wakiama*, leaving members of the latter group with the status merely of privileged individuals; for at present the Sonjo *wakiama* do not in any sense constitute a 'council'.

[2] There is no special Sonjo term for this category.

entitled—even one with large land holdings—and frequently two hours is sufficient to soak his plots. The water that is left over may then be distributed to the men who are without any special rights. A man in this latter category is usually required to pay a fee to his benefactor—a small quantity of honey if available, otherwise grain or even money.

A *mokiama* has to deal with the *wenamiji* as a corporate group in obtaining his water rights. If he is accepted and assigned a scheduled period for the use of irrigation water he agrees to provide a goat whenever the *wenamiji* ask for one, but no fixed tribute is set in advance. The goats are mostly used in ritual sacrifices and offerings which are supposed to benefit the whole community. The privileges of a *mokiama* cannot be purchased by just anyone who is willing to pay the required tribute, because there are only a limited number of these positions available. Therefore, the men who have achieved the status of *mokiama* guard their privileges jealously against competitors. Thus they are inclined to give political support to the *wenamiji* upon whom they are dependent for their water rights. In times of extreme water shortage it may be necessary to eliminate some of the *wakiama* in order to shorten the irrigation cycle and thus ensure that at least most of the crops are adequately irrigated. Thus the *wakiama* have no absolute assurance of future security in their water rights. They never meet or act as a corporate group, and the membership may change from time to time and fluctuate in numbers.

A client must obtain his water from an individual of one of the three superior categories; from his viewpoint it makes little difference as to which category the individual belongs. Wherever possible he applies to a close patrilineal relative for his water, usually to a father or brother. Lacking a relative to supply him with water, a client must compete with other clients for the water of non-relatives which may be available. If his resources of honey, grain, or money are relatively restricted he may find difficulty in obtaining as much water as his crops require. It will be obvious from this that a client is often in a precarious position with regard to irrigation water. When his attempts at negotiation fail and his crops are threatened with serious drought, he may be tempted to use water illegally by making a break in a water channel near one of his plots and flooding the plot at night. This form of self-help is said to be fairly common, though it is difficult to estimate the number of successful thefts of this kind. If detected by the *wenamiji*, a water thief is fined one goat, which is a relatively mild penalty compared to those for other forms of theft. Since water theft is usually actuated by dire necessity there is little moral stigma attached to the offence, as in the case of a man in Western society who steals bread for his starving family. My informant, Gidia, was detected and fined for stealing water during the period of his employment by me. This was the second time within a year that he had been so fined. He simply regarded this as unusually bad luck.

The *wenamiji* are the only group in the community exercising effective political authority, and thus they may be described as an oligarchy with respect to village government. Their political authority is derived in large measure from their control of irrigation water, for they have the power of depriving individuals of the water which is an absolute necessity for raising crops. This gives them an effective sanction for enforcing obedience to tribal laws and to their own administrative orders. The political role of the *wenamiji* and the nature of their political powers and authority will be analysed in chapter VIII.

Chapter V

FAMILY AND MARRIAGE

I T is assumed in the following discussion that the typical Sonjo family is monogamous. Although polygyny is practised, this form of marriage is relatively infrequent among the Sonjo as compared with many African societies. Therefore, the polygynous family will be dealt with as a special development or complication of the more usual monogamous family.

THE HOME

The partners of a monogamous marriage normally live together in a single house so long as their marriage lasts. When children are born, they also live in the same dwelling until the time arrives when, for various reasons, they leave their parental home. Thus the family as a mature institution, centred on a single home, is comprised of parents and children. Young married people desire children, among other reasons, to create a mature home and the normal domestic milieu of Sonjo society.

Although there are no reliable data concerning the average size of families, the Sonjo state that families are smaller at present than formerly. It is believed that the normal child-bearing capacity of a woman is eight children, and that this was quite commonly achieved in the old days, though now it has become rare. This alleged drop in the fertility rate of the tribe is generally attributed by the elders to current disregard for old customs and neglect of religious ritual, thus causing the disfavour of Khambageu with whom the ultimate control of fertility lies. There is actually some evidence of population decline, in the unoccupied house sites which are found at every village, but no clear indication of the cause of this decline. It seems unlikely that Sonjo families were formerly very much larger than at present in view of the predominance of monogamy and the tendency for births to be spaced at intervals of at least two and a half years. This tendency is the result of a rule forbidding sexual intercourse with a mother before her last child has been weaned. Other forms of birth control seem to be unknown in married life, as both partners desire as many children as possible. Both sons and daughters are desired, each bringing special benefits to the parents. Sons provide economic and social security in old age and are necessary to carry on the patrilineal line; while daughters relieve mothers of much of the back-breaking field work, and the goats that they bring to the family tend to balance the goats paid out at a son's marriage.

The house of a newly married couple is arranged inside as a single room. When the children of a family grow out of infancy, the back part of the house is partitioned off by a light wall as a private bedroom for the parents; the children then sleep in the main compartment of the house near the fireplace. Every individual sleeps on his own raised bed which is covered with a sleeping skin of goat, antelope, or cow hide. It is always warm in a house because of the goats, the fire, and the lack of ventilation, so that people do not require coverings while sleeping.

Meals are taken in the home, with the whole family eating together. The usual practice is to eat two hot meals a day—at noon and in the evening—with breakfast consisting of left over food eaten cold. The staple item at a meal is either a thick porridge made from sorghum or millet flour or sweet potatoes which may be boiled or roasted. A housewife grinds fresh flour before every meal, putting a pot of water on the fire in the meanwhile so that it will be ready for cooking the porridge when she has finished. A relish of some kind is eaten with the staple food, sometimes cooked meat or spinach, and at other times just goat's milk taken either fresh or clotted. Butter is added to the porridge or cooked relish when available. Beans and peas are mixed with other ingredients in the relish, or sometimes eaten in bulk as the main item of a meal. The Sonjo have no ritual food taboos, either for the whole tribe or individual clans, but certain foods are not considered edible by all or some of the people. Thus the flesh of wild pigs, though often available, is refused by many of the people; the Masai custom of drinking blood drawn from the vein of a bullock has been recently introduced, but it is considered repulsive by most people.

Each member of the family has his own plate and spoon, which are washed and put away after every meal. A woman has an extra set which she uses during her menstrual period and keeps hidden at other times. When a family has gathered for a meal and the food is ready, the porridge is dished up in the individual plates. The relish is served in a common bowl. The method of eating is for a person to take a spoonful of porridge, dip it in the relish, then put it in the mouth. Guests from the same village are not normally entertained at meals, but relatives from other villages are always offered food at meal time. It is not considered proper for a man to share food with anyone except close relatives or members of his own age-set, but this limitation does not apply to beer, which may be drunk in the company of any elders of the tribe. When sweet potatoes are plentiful, a few of them are boiled every day and kept on hand to give to young children as snacks between meals. Older children often steal sweet potatoes from the fields and roast and eat them secretly.

The roles played by boys and girls in the home are differentiated at an early age. Young boys, within a year or two after learning to walk, begin their careers as goatherds and are put in charge of those goats which are kept at the house. Several years later, at age six or seven, boys are normally sent out to stay at the goat camps located in the pastures some distance from the village, and thereafter they live at home only intermittently for short periods. After his initiation into a warrior age-set a boy can no longer be counted as a member of the domestic family, for he then sleeps away from home with his age-mates and takes most of his meals with them.

Daughters are trained at an early age to take care of younger children, thus leaving the mother free to cultivate her fields, and it is not uncommon to see a little girl of six or seven carrying a baby on her back. If a mother has no older daughter to help care for an infant, or if she is still nursing it, she carries it with her to the fields. There, all the infants are left in one place, and an older girl is appointed to look after them while the mothers work. Young daughters also learn to perform household tasks for their mother and are given miniature digging-sticks with which they practise the art of cultivation. As girls grow up they participate more and more in the field work, and are expected to be competent cultivators by the time of their marriage. Thus, from infancy onwards there is marked differentiation of activities according to sex, and small boys and girls are seldom seen playing together. This differentiation, however, is not rigid or enforced by formal sanctions. If necessity arises, a boy may be required to help his mother with tasks normally done by a daughter, and occasionally a girl is obliged to herd goats when there is no boy available for this work. Daughters live with their parents until marriage, but they frequently visit their grandparents, both paternal and maternal, and may stay with them for long periods of time.

The relationship between brothers and sisters is supposed to be warm and cordial throughout life, but not unduly intimate. There is no stereotyped avoidance between them, but as the two sexes follow divergent interests in childhood they are seldom together except on occasions when there is organized singing and dancing in the evening. After his initiation, a boy has little contact with his sisters, or for that matter with other girls, except of a formal or chaperoned nature. Situations of competition or rivalry rarely arise to strain the amiability existing between a brother and sister.

Brothers are often close companions. If their age difference is not great they probably share the management of a goat camp while young, and they may go through initiation together and belong to the same age-set. When there is a wide difference in age, the older brother shares with his father the task of teaching the younger brother. The cordial relationship between such brothers is likely to continue in adult life, for they are less likely to find themselves in a competitive situation than two brothers of the same age-set. The eldest son normally inherits the largest share of his father's wealth and may succeed to his father's position of authority until his brothers are all established in their own homes and the group breaks up into separate families. But if he is incompetent or lacks a sense of responsibility, the father may designate a younger son to succeed him. The principle of primogeniture is present but not strongly developed among the Sonjo.

After brothers have established families of their own and their father has died, the economic bonds which unite them as a family are weakened and their interests tend to diverge. If one brother is a *mwenamiji* on the village council, he is expected in certain situations to put council and village interests even above the interests of his adult brothers. Thus, one of my informants had an older brother who was a *mwenamiji*; occasionally the informant would obtain irrigation water from his brother, but usually he would have to look elsewhere for his water, because the brother would have used up his allotted water in meeting demands on him by people who were not his kinsmen.

Relations between parents and children are decorous and, in appearance at least, affectionate. A father is his son's chief tutor up to the age of initiation, and the two often appear to be companionable. A mother plays a similar role *vis-à-vis* her daughters. The authority of parents, particularly fathers, over their children is very great among the Sonjo and lasts until the parents' death. A high degree of obedience and respect is demanded of children. In the case of girls, the parental authority lasts until their marriage, after which there is little effective control over them by the parents, though respect is still demanded. A son is subject to his father's authority as an uninitiated boy and again as a young elder, but during the period of his warriorship, in the age-grades of junior and senior *batan*, a boy has little to do with his family, and the father's authority is accordingly diminished. A father is allowed to beat his sons for disrespect or disobedience. He can even strike a grown son who is himself head of a family, and the latter must submit. A father retains ultimate ownership of all goats and beehives in the family until his death. He normally divides these up among the sons as they marry, but they may not sell or otherwise dispose of them without his permission, and he may recall them if he wishes. The youngest son is traditionally supposed to be the parents' favourite child and to be treated more leniently. He is usually chosen for the honour of burying his father, who may also show him other favours during his lifetime. In a polygynous family the youngest son of the senior wife is supposed to be the father's favourite.

When a son or daughter is about to leave on a journey, or to start any enterprise involving danger or the risk of failure, a father customarily gives the child his formal blessing. If it is an important undertaking the mother too may bless the child. For the parents to withhold their blessing is tantamount to cursing the child. When this happens the child must make restitution with apologies, gifts, and exemplary behaviour. If the father remains obdurate the other leading elders of the ward will try to persuade him to forgive and bless the child. Discord in a family, if serious and prolonged, is regarded as a grave matter threatening the solidarity of ward and village.

BETROTHAL AND MARRIAGE

Traditionally, a man was not allowed to marry until he had passed through the warrior age-grades. Reckoning the age of initiation as from ten to seventeen years, and the period spent as a warrior in the two age-grades at fourteen years, this rule would set the minimum age for marriage at from twenty-four to thirty-one for men. The rule is no longer strictly observed, however, and young men who are still in the grade of senior warrior are now allowed to marry. The relaxation of this rule has resulted in a levelling off of the ages at which men marry, and also in a lowering of the average age of marriage. The change in this marriage rule is said to have been made recently, and there are some ambiguities in the social and economic position of a married youth who is still a warrior. Thus, as the proprietor of a house and fields, the husband of a wife, and perhaps the father of a child, his mode of life is bound to be quite different from that which tradition enjoins on the warriors; but he does not yet enjoy all the rights, nor is he required to assume the full responsibilities, of elderhood. In the case of girls, the only strict prerequisite for marriage is initiation, which includes circumcision. As this ceremony is only performed every seven years, some girls are initiated at the time of their puberty, while others may be several years younger or older.

Betrothal precedes marriage in most cases by many years, for Sonjo girls are customarily betrothed in early childhood or even infancy. A boy may also be quite young at the time of his betrothal, but he is always older than the girl, for in arranging the marriage the parents anticipate the future and aim at matching the ages of the two children so that when the boy

F

finally becomes an 'elder', and thus qualified for marriage, the girl will have just reached marriageable age herself. The betrothal agreement becomes final with the payment of bride-price, and these bride-price transactions will be described in the next section. At present there is considerable secrecy about betrothal arrangements because of a belief that these customs are illegal. Evidently a District Officer interpreted the betrothal of children as a form of 'child marriage' and announced to the elders that this was prohibited by Tanganyika law. Thus I found informants reluctant to discuss recent betrothals, though quite willing to tell about cases of some years ago.

The preliminary negotiations leading up to a betrothal may be carried out directly between the fathers of the boy and girl concerned or indirectly by go-betweens. After his suit has been tentatively accepted, the boy's father makes beer and brings it to the house of the girl's father, where the two men drink together and come to an agreement as to the size of the bride-price. A few days later the girl's father makes beer and invites the members of his own family and his wife's to come and confirm the agreement. At this gathering the people decide on the division of the bride-price. The next event is a feast given by the girl's father, for which beer is prepared and two goats are killed. The beer is drunk by the men of both families, but the meat is reserved for the men of the suitor's family and by four boys of his own age-set who also attend the feast. At this affair the boy's father is informed as to whom he should pay the bride-price goats.

When the bride-price payment is completed, the betrothal is celebrated with a feast provided by the girl's father at which beer and meat are served to members of both families as well as to the fiancé's four age-mates. This feast, which is private and does not involve the whole village, lasts four days and ends with a ceremony symbolizing the betrothal. A strip of fresh goat skin is pierced at both ends and the boy and girl each put their middle finger through a hole. The strip is then cut in two between the fingers. Then the girl and boy and the four age-mates are all marked on the forehead with a daub of goat-fat.

After the betrothal has been thus sealed, the affianced couple are expected to avoid one another as far as possible, or, if they chance to meet, must treat each other with exaggerated respect. The boy's brothers also treat the girl with avoidance or respect. The girl continues to live in the usual way with her father and mother, helping the latter with the housework and in the fields. From time to time her future mother-in-law may call upon her for help in some special task, and she is expected to respond. The father of one of my informants, Gidia, had died during the betrothal period, and the young man had in-herited several fields, which his mother continued to cultivate. Gidia also acquired several more fields through purchase with the money that he had earned in Arusha. This was too much land for his mother to work alone, and up to the time of the marriage his fiancée gave the greater share of her time to helping his mother with the cultivating. Later, after the mar-riage had taken place and the young couple had their own home, the roles of these two women were reversed; the mother then became the helper of the young wife, who assumes primary responsibility for the cultivation of the fields.

The Sonjo clans are strictly exogamous, and marriage be-tween all first cousins is forbidden. A man cannot marry the sister of his first wife, either contemporaneously as a second wife, or subsequently after his first wife has died or been di-vorced. Or, to state this rule differently, two sisters are never permitted to marry the same man. Neither can two sisters marry two brothers, for in that case if one brother died the surviving brother would not be allowed to inherit the widow because of the prohibition against a man marrying two sisters. It is forbidden to marry the daughter of an age-mate, but there is no bar to marrying his sister. The first marriage of a woman is nearly always with a man who comes from a different clan of the same village. My informants knew of no exceptions to this rule.

A census taken for tax purposes and completed at the village of Soyetu just before I left revealed that under twelve per cent of married men had more than one wife. Of these, only one man had three wives, the rest only two. The incentives for polygyny are largely economic. Thus, if a man has a large number of goats there is little in which he can invest them except as bride-price in multiple wives. Or if he should find himself in possession of an excessive amount of land through inheritance, it cannot be fully utilized unless he has a second wife to help cultivate it. Unlike many African societies, however, the Sonjo do not hold polygyny to be a highly desirable personal ideal; it is commonly stated that strife and discord between co-wives are inevitable, and that a polygynous household is not a harmonious one.

As the time for a marriage approaches, the bridegroom builds a new house with help from his father-in-law and men of his own ward. When this is finished, a final payment of the bride-price is made to the bride's father. The wedding events for a Sonjo wedding occupy four days—four being a favourite number among the Sonjo in ceremonial and ritual affairs. On the first day the groom sends four friends of his own age-set to call for the bride. She comes to the new house accompanied by a group of girls from her initiation class, bringing with her a new pair of sandals, four plates, eight horn spoons, and a sleeping skin, all this being a gift from her father. In the meanwhile the bride's father has prepared a feast of goat meat and invites the bridegroom and his four friends, who stay at that house feasting for the next four days. During this time the bride stays at the new house and puts it in order. Every night a number of women of the village gather at the house to sing. On the last day the new husband comes home and the marriage is consummated.

If a man marries a second wife, the wedding ceremonies, as well as the schedule of bride-price payments, is the same as for a first wife, provided it is the bride's first marriage. The time intervals, though, may be telescoped so that the whole series of events from betrothal to marriage takes place within a couple of months. Each wife must be provided with her own house. The first wife ranks as senior wife, regardless of her relative age. The husband makes her home his principal dwelling and keeps his belongings there. Her eldest son is the principal heir, even though he may be younger in age than his half brothers. The children of junior wives are supposed to acknowledge the rank of the senior wife by calling her 'mother', while her own children call junior wives 'little mother'.

BRIDE-PRICE

I have written elsewhere (Gray 1960) in some detail about Sonjo bride-price, attempting in that paper to interpret these customs in a comparative context of other African societies. Here I shall simply describe the customs without comparative reference to other societies.

The question of bride-price arises with the beginning of the negotiations which lead up to a betrothal. During the period of my field work, and the years immediately preceding, the bride-price for a girl's first marriage ranged from sixty to three hundred goats, the average being about one hundred. Before coming to an agreement as to the exact size of the bride-price, the two fathers consult with members of their respective circles of kinsmen, for the transaction will concern the kinsmen of both parties. After the bride-price is settled upon, and the engagement announced, the suitor's father is expected to make the full payment within two months, and he sets to work immediately to collect the necessary sum. The father usually provides about half the goats from his own herd. His own father (the fiancé's grandfather), if still living, is expected to make a substantial contribution, and in fact the old grandfather is still the legal owner of all the goats of the lineage, even though most of them are in the possession of his sons. The sons do not obtain full title of ownership to the goats until they inherit them upon his death. The father's brothers (the fiancé's uncles) are under strong obligation to provide most of the remaining goats needed to complete the bride-price. The boy's maternal grandfather does not contribute towards the bride-price but the mother's brothers are expected to make at least a token contribution of one or two goats each. Thus, in principle, the transaction concerns both sides of the boy's family. Once the bride-price has been paid it is never refunded, a fact which has implications which will be discussed below under the rules of divorce.

A poor man, whose brothers are usually also poor, may have difficulty in raising the bride-price for his son, and such a son may have to remain a bachelor until he finds the means of paying bride-price, sometimes as late as middle age. A man never contracts for a second marriage until after the first one has been completed, and seldom before his father has died. In a second marriage there is no prolonged betrothal period; the marriage follows soon after the payment of the bride-price. The husband himself then provides all or most of the bride-price, with his brothers helping him as they are able and wish to.

The division of the incoming bride-price among the girl's relatives is governed by more definite rules than in the case of the collection of the bride-price. The marriage histories of my informants indicate that these proportions are followed in the division: the girl's father receives approximately one quarter of the goats; another quarter is divided equally between her two grandfathers; another quarter is divided equally between the eldest brothers of her mother and father; the remaining quarter is divided among the other brothers of her father and mother, and their sisters may also receive one or two goats each if the bride-price is sufficiently large. The basic principle is that after the father's share has been subtracted, the remaining goats are divided equally between the relatives of the father and mother. That is, individuals of the same degree of relationship on either side of the family receive the same number of goats. The total number of goats claimed by each side, however, need not be equal. Thus if one of the parents has more brothers and sisters than the other, that side of the family would receive more goats altogether.

Just before the marriage ceremonies begin, a final payment of ten goats is made to the bride's father. This sum, which is invariable at all marriages, is divided among the bride's relatives on the same lines as the bride-price paid at the betrothal.

DEATH OF A MARRIAGE PARTNER

As was noted earlier, the bride-price which is paid to a girl's father at the time of the betrothal is never returned under any circumstances. Therefore the death of a betrothed girl represents a complete loss of the bride-price to the fiancé and his family, and the same is true of the death of a young wife, regardless of whether or not she has borne children. When a young man dies after his betrothal, but before his marriage, his eldest brother has an option to marry the girl himself, in which case he pays the girl's father twenty goats—double the usual payment at marriage. If this is not done, the right to marry the girl may be sold to another man for thirty goats, which are divided among the dead boy's father and brothers. The buyer is also required to pay twenty goats to the girl's father. This transaction is regarded in some respects as a divorce, and therefore the *wenamiji* collect seven goats from the man who marries her—the customary fee for divorce and remarriage.

When a husband dies his wife is inherited by the eldest surviving brother. He then becomes the father of the surviving children, but their exact status depends on their ages and also on whether their paternal grandfather (the dead man's father) is still living. If the grandfather is dead the father would already have inherited his share of the property, which would later be divided among the children when they came of age. But if the grandfather were still living, the father would not yet have acquired outright ownership of his property, which would then revert to the family estate. In that case the children would ultimately look to their father's brother for a share of his property.

If the surviving children are already grown up, and particularly if some of the sons are already married, the mother does not actually live with her husband's brother as his wife. She continues to live in her own house, and with her children constitutes a separate family. If the eldest son is already married and has established a stable home, he may act as head of the family and look after the interests of his brothers and sisters until they come of age. The mother then lives as a widow and looks only to her children for protection and support. Still another arrangement is sometimes made when the dead man has no brothers who are in a position to take responsibility for the family. The surviving widow may move with her small children to the homestead of her own brother, who then assumes the role of father to the children. The children may even be adopted into the mother's clan, especially if surviving members of the father's lineage have little interest in them. When this happens the men of the mother's lineage are responsible for providing bride-price so that the boys can get wives, and they receive the bride-price that is paid when the daughters are betrothed.

DIVORCE

Divorce customs are important for an understanding of Sonjo social structure, because they bring some of the key relationships into sharp relief and indicate the nature and strength of these relationships. A broken engagement is dealt with by Sonjo law in much the same way as a divorce. If a young man does not wish to marry his fiancée he can send her a broken twig, which signifies his decision. The girl is then free to accept another suitor, who has only to pay the fiancé the original bride-price and may then marry the girl. The girl herself can also break the engagement if she can find an alternative suitor who is willing to pay back the bride-price. If her fiancé finds another man who will buy his marriage rights, the girl is obliged to accept the change unless she can find someone more to her liking within a reasonable period of time. Whoever finally marries the girl must make the regular marriage payment of ten goats to her father before the marriage, and he must also pay a fee of seven goats to the *wenamiji* of the village.

Instead of 'selling' the betrothal rights to a girl, it is more usual to exchange her with another man who also has a fiancée whom he does not want to marry. If the two bride-prices were the same an even trade is made of the two girls. If one was larger than the other, the difference in goats must be made good to the man with the more costly fiancée. When an exchange of brides is made both men are taxed with a divorce fee by the *wenamiji*, but only four goats are collected from each one, the other three being waived on condition of good behaviour. If either man is later guilty of transgressing customary law he is immediately required to pay the remaining three goats. In every case where there is a change in betrothal partners, the girl's father must give his approval.

After her marriage a woman is comparatively free from the control of her father or other relatives, and they do not directly intervene in any divorce proceedings. Where there are no children, the principles of divorce are the same as in breaking an engagement. Either the husband or the wife may initiate the divorce. A woman usually leaves her husband and goes to her father's home or to a brother. The husband cannot make her return by force. In time, if she persists in her demands, he will indicate his permission for the divorce by accepting bride-price from another man who wants to marry her. These goats, which are his means of obtaining another wife, should equal the original bride-price.

If the husband initiates a divorce he seeks a buyer for his wife who will pay him the original bride-price. The wife is always given a grace period for finding a more desirable second husband before she is required to marry the man found by her husband. The new husband must belong to a different clan from the first, and of course he cannot belong to the woman's clan because of exogamy; these restrictions limit the possibility of finding another husband in the same village. It is possible, and indeed the usual practice, for a woman's second husband to be a man of another village. A man can also sell his wife out of the tribe to a Masai if he is determined to divorce her and no Sonjo husband can be found for her. In these divorces and remarriages no payment is made to the woman's father. In addition to repaying the bride-price, the new husband only pays the fee of seven goats to the *wenamiji*. As in the case of betrothed couples, two men may exchange wives and adjust the difference in bride-price between them. Three-cornered exchanges of wives are also practised. In that case A marries B's wife, B marries C's wife, and C marries A's wife. Again there is an adjustment so that each man received the equivalent of his original bride-price payment.

When children have been born in a family, there are new factors to be considered in arranging a divorce. According to Sonjo law, children must always stay with their mother. Therefore when a mother is divorced and remarried, her children go with her and are adopted by the new husband. The repayment of the bride-price is the same as for a childless wife. The children, however, are valued at four goats apiece, which must be paid to their father by the new husband. Sometimes two men exchange wives and children, and then the number of children, as well as the original bride-price of their wives, must be taken into account in settling up.

The children of a mother who has been divorced break most of their kinship bonds with members of their father's lineage. Thereafter they are not barred from marriage with people of his clan, but only with the father's close relatives—his own children and the children of his brothers and sisters. The father himself loses all rights over his children by a former wife and has no further obligations towards them. The native law on this point is clear: children belong to their mother's legal husband. He has full rights over them and assumes the responsibility of providing bride-price for the stepsons' wives. Property inheritance is also through the stepfather. The children are assimilated to his clan and automatically acquire the same kinship bonds with his blood relatives as his own children have. Their relationships with their mother's family, though, remain unchanged.

The preceding account assumes that the children are quite young, in which case there is no ambiguity in their position. Rights over young children are unequivocally vested in their paterfamilias whether or not he is also their genitor. But when the children are older the situation may be more complex. If a daughter had already been betrothed before her mother's divorce, the bride-price which was paid for her is kept by her father, her first husband. Factors such as this would be considered by the two husbands at the time of the divorce when settling the question of payment for children and the like. However, as it rarely happens that a mother with older children is divorced, these complications seldom arise.

EXTRAMARITAL SEX RELATIONS

In judging the seriousness of extramarital sex offences, the Sonjo distinguish sharply between offences which involve circumcised and uncircumcised persons. An illicit pregnancy involving an uncircumcised boy or girl is regarded as a grave ritual offence, imparting a permanent stigma to both individuals concerned. Circumcision must be performed before the pregnancy results in birth. The guilty youth is required to expiate his sin by clearing a patch of forest far from the village and planting a field of sorghum there; he must cultivate it until the grain is ripe and then leave it unharvested. In every case the boy is required to marry the pregnant girl, and she usually remains his wife for life; for the ritual contamination which she acquires renders her permanently unfit to be married by another Sonjo. If the husband divorces her, she must be remarried outside the tribe. If the putative father cannot be found, the girl is generally sold to the Masai, as there is no social position for such a woman permanently to occupy among the Sonjo. If the girl was already betrothed before her pregnancy, her engagement is broken and her paramour must restore the bride-price to her original fiancé.

Before a boy is initiated he is not legally responsible for his acts, and if he becomes involved in an illicit pregnancy he is not fined or required to pay compensation: the offence is largely a ritual one. But if an initiated man has an affair with an initiated girl he is fined twelve goats by the *wenamiji*. When an initiated girl becomes illicitly pregnant the ritual offence is less serious. She must undergo a purification ceremony before the birth of her child, but neither she nor the infant acquire permanent ritual impurity. If the girl was betrothed or married, the man responsible for her pregnancy must pay compensation of six goats to the fiancé or husband, as the case may be, and is fined another six goats by the *wenamiji*. These affairs do not necessarily result in a broken engagement or divorce. The fiancé or husband usually accepts the illegitimate child as his own. It is difficult to prove that a pregnancy of a wife is illicit unless the woman herself confesses. It is believed that such a pregnancy will result in a difficult childbirth unless the woman confesses and proper purification ceremonies are performed before the birth. Therefore, adultery is often suspected in cases of difficult or prolonged labour, and the woman is encouraged to confess and name the guilty man.

WATURI

Smiths and potters and their families are forced to practise clan endogamy because of the strict taboo prohibiting other Sonjo from marrying Waturi. The Waturi themselves are quite willing to marry outside of their clan, and sometimes marry Masai, but the marriage of a Moturi is generally with a fellow clansman. At present there is a disparity in the sex ratio and in the economic position of men and women in this clan. The demand for locally made iron goods has decreased, while the demand for pottery (made by the women of the clan) remains unchanged. Consequently some of the men have left the tribe, usually finding work among the Masai, and those who remain are not fully employed at their craft. As a result of the surplus of women, the incidence of polygyny is higher among the Waturi than among the general population, and the bride-price is much lower—eight to ten goats as against sixty to three hundred for the other clans. Marriage between cousins —strictly prohibited for other Sonjo—is the usual practice for the Waturi, either cross-cousins or parallel cousins being eligible for marriage without preference.

Sexual intercourse as well as marriage is prohibited between Waturi and other Sonjo, but there may have been periods of laxness in observing this injunction. According to the myth of Waturi origin, a smith and a potter arrived at Sonjo and began practising their crafts. They begat children, who were not able to marry because they were full brothers and sisters. The daughters then 'walked' with other men of the tribe and became pregnant. The children born of these affairs were permitted to marry, as they were only cousins. This myth implies that the Sonjo prohibition against intercourse with Waturi women has not always been observed. More recently a similar laxness is said to have crept in, until a point was reached only a few years ago where three men decided to marry Waturi girls. The first of these was a brother of one of my informant's step-mother (his mother's co-wife). About a year after his marriage he died suddenly, and shortly afterwards his sister (the step-mother) died. These deaths were universally interpreted as a supernatural punishment for breaking the taboo. But despite this warning, two other youths also married Waturi girls. One of them died a month after his marriage, and the other became seriously sick but recovered. The village council then inter-vened and ordered that the Waturi women be sent home immediately. An atonement ritual involving large-scale offer-ings and sacrifices to Khambageu was then performed to purify the tribe of the guilt of these unlawful marriages. At the present time the taboo is strictly observed.

INHERITANCE

The principal assets of a man which may be passed on to his heirs after death are real property, including house sites and cultivated fields; personal property, such as livestock and bee-hives; rights over women and children; and hereditary social position. The first two categories are normally inherited by the sons according to the same general rule of division: the eldest son takes the biggest share, and the other sons divide the remainder more or less equally. A man's wives and children are inherited by his eldest brother, never by his sons. The only special social position that is regularly hereditary is that of *mwenamiji*—membership on the village council. Succession to this position may be either by a brother or a son. The priest-hood of the tribe is organized as a separate clan which in many ways resembles ordinary clans. Therefore the office of priest is acquired through patrilineal succession. The priesthood will be discussed in chapter VII.

House sites are not regarded as individual property but belong to the whole clan. A lineage normally has customary rights to build houses in a certain section of a ward, and sons inherit the sites of their father; but these sites can not be leased or sold, and the clan leader can reassign unused sites to a different family. When a houseowner dies, his widow normally continues to live in his house, either as the wife of the brother who inherits her or independently with her children. Cultivated plots are individually owned and can be leased to outsiders if not needed. This transaction virtually amounts to a sale, with the provision that the seller has the option of buying back the plot for the same price. The land needs of different families vary from time to time, and the leasing system makes it pos-sible to adjust to these needs. A young man requires cultivation plots for the first time when he marries; his father turns some of his own plots over to him at that time, or he may then lease other available land. The son, however, does not acquire full ownership to the land until his father dies. An eldest son in-herits more land than his brothers, and if it is a large family, the latter may have to use their own resources to lease enough land for their needs.

In the case of goats, the eldest son inherits about half of the total, or less than half if there are many sons, with the other sons dividing up the rest. The youngest son sometimes receives a slightly larger share than his older brothers. Step-sons, or any sons that a man may have adopted, such as a

sister's son, have full rights with his own sons, and inherit
their share of his property according to their positions of
seniority. Beehives are divided among the sons in the same way
as goats. Because the gathering of honey is the work of agile
young men, hives are divided up as soon as the father starts
ageing, but all the honey gathered from them is given to him
while he lives. Honey is a valuable trade commodity and an
elder's prestige is partly determined by the amount of honey
beer he can supply. By traditional Sonjo law, a son is not
allowed to make honey beer while his father is still alive.

A man's wives are inherited by his eldest surviving brother,
who may take the widow as his wife and adopt the children, or
may allow the widow and children to live separately as an
independent family and simply act as guardian and trustee.
He may also sell the widow or exchange her for the wife of
another man. If there are no surviving brothers of her husband
she may move to the homestead of her own lineage, and her
brother may adopt the children as his own. A wife has no permanent ownership rights in her husband's property. She can
continue to cultivate her fields if she becomes the wife of her
husband's brother, or if she has sons who will eventually inherit them. But an older widow without sons may find herself
without the means of subsistence and be forced to return to
her brother's lineage for support. The food supplies stored in
a house or standing in a field, though normally controlled by
a wife, belong ultimately to her husband, and in case of a
divorce they remain with him. When parents become old and
helpless it is obligatory on their sons to support them. An aged
father is still legally the owner of all his sons' property, even
that which they may have acquired through their own efforts,
and he is thus in a position to demand the necessities of life
from them. In the case of a mother, the obligation to support
her in old age is a moral one, but it is usually done willingly
because of the normal affection between mothers and sons.

Succession to the position of *mwenamiji* is governed by rules
of inheritance; other positions of authority are elective in
nature, either wholly, as for age-grade leaders, or partly, as
for ward leaders, where both seniority and individual compe-
tence are considered in making the choice. At the same time
that a new *mwenamiji* succeeds to his office, one of his brothers

may establish his claim to succeed him. If this is not done, the man's eldest son will automatically succeed him.

To illustrate further these rules, the history of inheritance in the family of my informant Gidia will be summarized. Gidia's father, Budwai, died a few years ago leaving two widows. The senior wife had borne four sons and four daughters and the junior wife four sons and one daughter. Not long before his death he had sold a third wife and two children to a Masai, who had paid sixty goats for the wife and forty for the children. This transaction was made primarily for the benefit of his sons, so that there would be more goats to divide among fewer heirs. Gidia was the youngest son of the senior wife.

Because of the unusually large number of sons, the section of the ward traditionally occupied by this lineage became crowded, and for that reason Gidia built his house in a new section of the village which had previously been outside the fortifications. The possibility of now doing this has taken away the scarcity value of traditional house sites. Budwai had nine fields altogether, of which the eldest son inherited three; Gidia received two fields, one *magare* and one *hura*, and five other sons received one field each. The youngest son did not inherit any land, but it is understood that his brothers will help him acquire fields when he marries. Gidia was designated as the son who should bury his father, and for this reason he received the largest share of the inheritance after the eldest son.

Of the three hundred goats left by Budwai, the eldest son inherited over one hundred, the other sons about twenty-five each, and Gidia, by virtue of his favoured position, received thirty. Gidia was a *motan* at the time of his father's death and therefore was not in a position to tend his goats, so his eldest brother took charge of these goats until Gidia's marriage. Budwai's sixty beehives were divided in the same proportions as the goats: the eldest son took a third of them, and the younger sons received equal shares of the remaining hives.

Gidia's mother stayed on in her house with her younger children, and her eldest son acted as head of the family. His wife died leaving two small children, who are now being cared for by their grandmother. Budwai's junior wife died shortly after his own death. She was the sister of one of the men who married *Waturi* girls. Budwai was a *mwenamiji*, and when he died his eldest son succeeded him as a member of the council. This involved paying an initiation fee equivalent to seven goats. The eldest son of the junior wife contributed one goat towards the initiation fee and thus established his claim to be next in line to inherit the membership.

LINEAGE STRUCTURE

The effective patrilineal group is best defined by the rules governing the transfer of property. This group normally includes a father and his sons. Brothers are bound together by their common dependence on their father, while he is living, and by mutual responsibility for taking care of one another's children should one of the brothers die. When an old father dies his sons obtain full possession of their property. Later, when their own children are all grown up, there are no longer strong economic bonds among them and they tend to break up into separate homesteads. This small patrilineal group, held together mainly by economic bonds, is the fundamental building block of Sonjo social structure. There is no formal alignment of lineage groups into larger lineage segments short of the entire clan. The range of kinship that is specifically recognized is narrow, and genealogical knowledge is shallow—some men do not know the names of their patrilineal grandfathers.

The structure and functions of the clan will be discussed in chapter VIII. Here I shall only state that it is conceived of as a patrilineal descent group; therefore clan-mates think of themselves as related to one another. This belief forms the basis of the rule of clan exogamy. The clan is not systematically segmented into a descending order of lineages, but is essentially an aggregate of small lineage groups as these were defined in the preceding paragraph. As we shall see later, the clan is structurally weak when compared with other social alignments.

Chapter VI

AGE-GRADES

LIKE many other tribes in East Africa (cf. Prins 1953) the Sonjo organize the youths of the tribe, within the age limits of adolescence to young adulthood, into formal groups which are military in nature. The present chapter will be devoted mainly to a description of this military age-group organization, with briefer notice of the organization of younger and older age-groups.

There has been some controversy over the terminology of age organizations (cf. Radcliffe-Brown 1929; Prins 1953 : 9–12). This need not concern us here, for our present task is to study the nature of Sonjo age organization, rather than comparative problems. The definition of 'age-grade' proposed by Radcliffe-Brown (1929 : 21)—'recognized divisions of the life of an individual as he passes from infancy to old age'—is adequate for our purposes. The Sonjo recognize three major age-grades: the first encompasses the life of a boy up to the time of his circumcision; an individual in this grade is referred to as a *kijori* (pl. *vijori*). The second starts with an initiation ceremony occurring shortly after circumcision and lasts for about fourteen years; a young man in this age-grade is called a *motana* (pl. *batana*). After a man graduates from his warrior grade, he becomes known as a *montomonkolo* (pl. *bamolankolo*), which may be translated simply as 'elder'. Besides these major divisions, a transitional grade lasting from circumcision to initiation—a period of one or two years—is formally recognized, and the members are given the term *lebardani* (borrowed from the word *laibartan*, used by the Masai in a similar context [Leakey 1930 : 191]). The warrior age-grade is subdivided into two divisions, as will be explained further below.

There is no ceremony marking the entrance of an individual into the grade of *vijori*. A boy simply grows from an infant to a *kijori* as he becomes capable of herding duties at the age of five or six. Thereafter his life is largely devoted to tending

G

goats until he is initiated into the warrior grade. During this time he becomes thoroughly grounded in animal husbandry, being taught the art by his father and older brothers, but mainly by older *vijori*. For the first two or three years a boy is charged with tending the household herd of female animals and their young. After that he is entrusted with the main herd and is sent for some weeks at a time to stay at the goat camps located at a distance of up to eight miles from the village. The goat owners of the same clan (or ward) tend to build their goat camps in the same general area of the pasture, but this is not an invariable rule. At any rate, the herd-boys from different camps visit one another frequently and thus become acquainted and exchange information and lore.

The older *vijori* carry small bows and arrows and use them for shooting partridges and guinea fowl, which is the main source of meat in their diet. Some adult of a boy's family, often his father, visits the camp each day and brings cooked food, but the boys are left much to their own resources. Their behaviour is modelled on that of the warriors, and to some extent their organization is integrated with the military system. Thus when a leopard or hyena seizes a goat or threatens to attack a camp at night, the news is relayed from camp to camp by pre-arranged signals and is soon known at the village, whereupon a company of warriors sets off immediately to hunt down the animal. In former times the herd-boys were exposed to attack by Masai raiding parties. Those who occupied out-lying camps are said to have spent their nights up in trees for safety. Warning signals consisted in imitations of animal or bird cries. Thus the boys served as an auxiliary to the military force by acting as additional sentries. In short, the life of the *vijori*, centred on goats, was relatively self-contained; it was austere and rigorous and prepared them for the military duties to come.

CIRCUMCISION AND INITIATION

Circumcision is performed on boys[1] between the ages of about nine and fifteen. The ceremonies in the circumcision-initiation

---

[1] Sonjo girls are circumcised in the same cycle as boys, but since data on this subject are incomplete it will not be discussed here.

cycle takes place on three consecutive years in the same general season of each year. The last cycle started at Kheri in the rainy season of 1953 with the circumcision of the first group of boys. The second group was circumcised in the same season in 1954. A year later both groups were initiated and became *batana*. The first circumcision group is comprised of the older boys and the second group of the younger ones. A father has to make the decision, in the case of a son who is near the lower age limit, whether to have the boy circumcised as one of the youngest members of the second group, or to have him wait until the next cycle and have him circumcised as one of the oldest of the first group. The ages which I cite in years are only approximations, because the qualification for circumcision is based on developmental rather than chronological age. Since the interval between initiations is seven years, we can calculate that the age difference at circumcision between the youngest and oldest boys is six years, while the age span of the combined group at initiation is seven years on the average: the oldest boys at circumcision are two years older when they are initiated, while the youngest boys are only one year older. Thus the age at initiation ranges from about ten to seventeen.

All the villages circumcise their candidates in the same years —which are automatically determined by counting from the year of the last initiation—but on different dates, which are decided by the elders of the village. The older boys are anxious to have the operation performed on them as soon as possible, and when the elders seem to be delaying unduly in setting a date they sometimes try to precipitate the event by circumcising themselves. Two boys at Soyetu attempted self-circumcision at the recent cycle and this induced the elders to order the ceremony immediately. All the boys of a village are circumcised on the same day if possible, otherwise two days are taken. Two circumcisers (*bamorati*, sing. *momorati*) usually work at the same time. This task may be performed by any elder who has learned the art, and the office is not a ritual one. They are paid a fee by each father of one gourd of honey beer and one shoulder of goat meat. Each boy is circumcised in front of his own house, supported by his mother's brother and observed by other male relatives and friends of the family. The father sits inside the house with a few old friends drinking beer nonchalantly. It is considered a disgrace to the father as well as to the boy if the candidate cries out loud with pain when the foreskin is cut. Prior to the operation the boy is usually promised several goats by his father and by other male relatives as well; these are later delivered to the boy as requested to be used in ceremonial feasts of the warriors. But if the boy cries out these promises are nullified, and thus he may be chagrined when he is unable to produce his share of the goats at feasts.

After his circumcision a boy is secluded in his house for two days. Then he leaves the house early in the morning to join his confreres and go into the forest for the day. Each boy has a bow and a supply of arrows, prepared before the ceremony, with which he shoots birds and small animals. The birds are stuffed and tied to the edge of wooden hoop which is worn as a ceremonial headdress at dances.[1] For every bird shot he makes a notch on his bow; a rat entitles him to four notches and a snake to thirty. In the evening the boys return to the village, and every morning thereafter for the next three months they leave the village early, before people are abroad, to shoot birds in the forest. These trophies are symbols of prowess and are exhibited with pride by the boys. The informant Gidia states that after his circumcision he completely filled one bow with over a hundred notches and half of a second bow. However, if any of the boys are bad marksmen or very unlucky, their comrades help them out so that they have at least a few bird skins to wear on their headdresses. In each ward of the village one house is set aside for the circumcised boys of the ward to sleep in. During this period of ceremonial hunting these boys eat together of food brought to them by their parents. In the evenings they learn special songs which they sing at their own initiations, and later at other ceremonies in which their age-set participates.

Circumcision confers a new ritual status on a Sonjo boy— for one thing, he is no longer strictly forbidden sexual intercourse on the grounds of being impure—and qualifies him for initiation into the warrior class. He is now a *lebardani* instead

[1] This custom seems to have been borrowed from the Masai (cf. Leakey 1930 : 190). Since no circumcision occurred during my visit, I was not able to witness these events, but after leaving the Sonjo I saw recently circumcised Masai youths wearing headdresses of stuffed birds exactly like those described by Sonjo informants.

of a *kijori*; as such he is subject to mild hazing by the *batana* and is expected to obey their orders and do errands for them. After the ceremonial hunting period is finished he goes back to his old duties of herding goats for one or two years until his initiation. This is one of the most important of Sonjo ceremonies. The fathers of all the candidates slaughter goats for feasting and prepare large quantities of beer; the warriors of the two sub-grades have feasts and ceremonies to celebrate their own promotion to higher grades, which coincides with the initiation of the candidates. The candidates themselves are given instruction in the duties of warriors; then they are shaved and prepared to participate in two ceremonial dances on consecutive days. On the first day they discard their headdresses, the birds being given to young children to play with, and their old garments, which are given to younger *vijori* and replaced with new apparel—cloths nowadays, though formerly the warrior costume was a skin skirt. On the second day they are formally acknowledged to be warriors—*batana*. Initiation ceremonies are performed separately at the different villages, but all in the same year and in close succession.

BATANA

All the boys in the tribe who are initiated in the same year constitute a closed group of people who are given a distinctive name and recognize special bonds among themselves which last the rest of their lives. I shall call this group an 'age-set', as it falls within the scope of the definition given to that term by Radcliffe-Brown (1929 : 21): 'A recognized and sometimes organized group consisting of persons (often male persons only) who are of the same age.' Despite Radcliffe-Brown's (1929 : 21) expressed dissatisfaction with the word 'class' I shall also use this term in the form 'warrior class' to distinguish the formally organized warriors of a village from other socio-economic classes of men. Thus my terminology for Sonjo age organization includes three concepts. (1) AGE-GRADES are the unchanging institutional forms, a pattern of roles which are filled by generation after generation. The warrior age-grade is subdivided into junior and senior grades with the respective titles of *batana barirage* (sing. *motana moriri*) and *batana bakolage* (sing. *motana mokolo*). (2) An AGE-SET is a group of men who are initiated in the same year; thereafter they pass from one age-grade to the next together as an organized group. (3) The term AGE-CLASS is used only with reference to the warrior class considered as one of several classes into which Sonjo society is stratified. The warrior class at any one time is composed of two age-sets occupying the respective grades of junior and senior *batana*.

A Sonjo age-set not only extends through the whole tribe, but is conceived of as encompassing other tribes as well, or at least of being synchronized with the age-grade systems of other tribes. Each age-set has its own name, but the name is not finally decided upon until several years after the set is formed. Some sets fail to agree on a final choice and are known by two alternative names. Nearly all the names are Sonjo versions of Masai names, though the meanings of these names, if they originally had meanings, are not generally known. The age-grade system is not cyclical like the Kipsigis system (Prins, 1953 : 35) but each age-set has a different name with no repetitions. The names of the last eleven age-sets are known to a number of the elders. These are listed below, starting with the oldest and giving the alternative names for those sets possessing them.

1. Olnyamburete
2. Oligikurukuru
3. Olmarabuta (the oldest age-set with members still living)
4. Oltalala
5. Simbau/Ndyunken
6. Olgishoni
7. Lobiro
8. Olobilieni/Saba
9. Olometoi/Ngurindo
10. Olmodidieni/Olkalikali
11. Oldetieni (initiated in 1955)

The Sonjo claim that when travelling through Masailand individuals can demand hospitality from Masai whose age-sets are synchronized with theirs. Corresponding data from the Masai which might confirm these claims are lacking, however.

Although the age-sets are tribal in scope, there is no formal structuring of a whole set. Members from different villages recognize bonds of brotherhood among themselves and frequently exchange visits, especially at a village festival when small delegations of warriors from other villages come in formal costume and join their age-mates in dancing. There is no leader for the whole set. A Sonjo age-set may be compared to a national fraternal organization with organized local (village) chapters but no national headquarters. The village chapters of an age-set are organized in slightly different ways at Kheri and Soyetu—the two villages from which data were gathered on this question. At Kheri a leader for the whole village is elected within a year or so after initiation. He is presented with a ceremonial club as a symbol of his office. Although he may be deposed for bad behaviour, he normally holds this position for life. When he dies the surviving members of the age-set elect a new leader who succeeds to the office and inherits the ceremonial club. As successive leaders die, the office is passed on to survivors until all the members are dead. The village leader has real powers of command over his warrior age-mates and represents them in conferring with the leader of the second age-set and the *wenamiji* or ruling council of elders. The age-set is divided into four companies—corresponding to the four wards of the village—each of which elects its own leader who serves as a lieutenant under the village leader. At Soyetu the age-set is divided into three companies, each representing two village wards. There is no paramount leader for the whole village, but each company elects its own leader, who receives a ceremonial club, holds office for life, and is succeeded by a surviving age-mate when he dies, in the same manner as the village leader at Kheri. The whole age-set is ruled jointly by a council of these three leaders.

In discussing the activities and duties of the warrior class it is necessary to distinguish between pre-European conditions and the present situation. Traditionally the primary function of the warriors was to provide protection against Masai raids, but since the establishment of the Pax Britannica this function no longer exists. First we shall consider the age-sets as they operated in the traditional system, and then indicate some of the changes that have ensued in recent times. An age-set at each village was divided into three or four companies, so the two sets together supplied six or eight companies of warriors. Only the oldest men of the tribe have had the experience of serving as warriors when the age-sets were still carrying out traditional military duties. Piecing together the scattered information obtained from them, it appears that at least three companies were always on duty in a village; one company stayed at the guardhouse and was charged with guarding the village gateway, or both gates in those villages with two. Two other groups acted as scouts; they left the village in opposite directions and patrolled the area within fifteen or twenty miles of the village, spying out Masai movements in the region and giving warning of the approach of Masai raiding parties. A system of vocal signals made it possible to transmit news of approaching Masai very rapidly. Then the goats were hurriedly brought in from the pastures, everyone retired inside the village fortifications, and the gates were closed. The patrolling companies stayed outside to observe the enemy—for days at a time, if a siege ensued, subsisting on game which they were skilled in hunting.

During an attack both the outer and inner gates were manned by archers crouching on the platforms above the gates. Sentries were posted all around the inside of the thorn hedge to guard against enemy raiders who might try to cut a path through it. If the gates appeared in danger of being breached, the elders brought house doors, made of heavy planks, and constructed redoubts at elevated points in the village for a last-ditch stand. The elders state that none of the present villages was ever conquered by the Masai, but it is believed that some of the abandoned villages were overpowered, though the details of these historical events are not known.

It is not clear from the accounts of elders how the duties of the two age-sets differed. The youngest of the warriors were still boys, obviously incapable of serious military duties; the average age difference between the two sets amounted to seven years, and there was also a big difference in training and experience. These differences were very likely taken into account in assigning duties to the various companies. Occasionally some of the older warriors would lay plans to ambush a small group of Masai warriors. First they would scout in the neighbourhood of a Masai *manyatta* or warrior encampment until they were familiar with the daily movements of the Masai. Then they would lie in wait along a frequented path and shoot the Masai with poisoned arrows. If they brought home the Masai weapons as proof of the deed they were received as heroes and given the title of *khajuri*—the highest honour existing among the Sonjo. On returning to their village they would first sing a special song outside the gate. The elders would come out and administer a rigorous purification rite. They were then given long withes decorated with tufts of feathers on the end to carry as symbols of their valour. There was rejoicing and dancing in the village, and the heroes were given ten goats as a gift. Later they toured the other villages and at each place they were presented with ten goats. The goats were consumed at victory feasts celebrated by the whole warrior class of the heroes' village.

One of the tasks of the junior *batana* was to keep the fortified village gates in good repair. The defensive fortifications have not been needed for a long time, but the gates are still kept up and are now regarded somewhat as sacred relics. Each new set of junior *batana* is required to rebuild them some time during the seven years served in that grade. Informants who were initiated in 1948 state that their set spent two years collecting timbers and then rebuilt the gates. The 1955 set had not yet started on this task six months after their initiation. In the old days the gates offered the only means of leaving or entering a village. Sometimes the *wenamiji* wished to prohibit headstrong warriors from raiding Masai camps. They would solemnly attach a charm to the gate which was supposed to bring disaster to anyone who passed through to start on a forbidden journey. This is said to have been effective in preventing unauthorized raids.

Traditionally a man was not allowed to marry until he had finished his military service and become an elder. During this time he was free of economic responsibilities and had little to do with his family or other sections of the population outside the age-sets. The warriors of each company built their own house which served them as a barracks and in which they slept. For their meals the whole company would call each time at a different house in the ward, stopping at all the houses in rotation. In effect, the company resembled a military force billeted among the civilian population of the ward. About half of the warrior class would be free of routine duties at any one time. Much of this free time would be spent in temporary camps in the forest several miles away from the village. Such a camp was surrounded by a zariba of thorn branches, with only a narrow tunnel for an opening, for there was (and still is) danger of marauding Masai warriors raiding the camp for goats. For this reason sentries were posted on the tracks leading to the camp.

These forest camps are still conducted in the traditional way so they can be described in the present tense. The main object is to feast on goat meat. Usually the different companies plan their feasts separately, but for very special occasions, such as the annual Mbaribari festival, the entire age-set of a village may form one large camp. The goats are produced by individual members of the company or age-set. At the time of his circumcision, as was mentioned earlier, each boy is promised a number of goats for this purpose by his father's father (if still alive), his father, his father's brothers, and his mother's brothers. The boy later demands these goats as he is called upon to produce them for feasts. When his circumcision goats are used up he begs more goats as needed from his father and other senior male relatives. A second essential ingredient of these feasts is the infusions of certain barks and roots which have narcotic effects of different kinds. These herbal infusions are mixed with meat broth and drunk. Depending on the kind and amount taken, the individual experiences effects ranging from mild euphoria to extreme excitement, delirium, and even convulsions. The usual programme at a feast is to spend the day at the camp eating meat and drinking broth doctored with herbs. Then in the evening the warriors come to the village and dance at a ward plaza, though at an important festival they may dance in the village plaza. It is expected that one or two individuals will have seizures of frenzy or convulsions, or run amuck in some way.[1] When this happens their comrades seize them and hold them down until they come to their senses. Taken in moderate doses, these herbs are supposed to impart strength, endurance, and courage to those who imbibe them, which is the traditional reason for their use.

[1] Masai warriors make similar use of stimulating and narcotic herbs (cf. Fox 1930 : 454), and the Sonjo may have borrowed the custom from them.

Ideally, the warriors were supposed to lead celibate lives, and the junior *batana* are actually expected to adhere strictly to this rule. They are urged to take certain herbs which are believed to cool sexual passions. The senior *batana*, who have some disciplinary authority over their juniors, take note of any infractions of this rule and fine the offender a goat. The seniors themselves are allowed more latitude in this matter and often develop liaisons with married women of the village. If such an affair becomes public, the *motana* involved is fined a goat by the leader of his set. If caught in a compromising situation by a husband, a warrior is subject to the same penalty as a married man.

According to older informants, the military system began to break down after the First World War with the establishment of British administration, and the activities and functions of the warrior classes are now quite different from the traditional ones. Two of these changes may be singled out as especially significant for the social structure. (1) Senior *batana* are now allowed to marry. This means that they no longer live together in a barracks but must have houses of their own where they live with their wives. They must obtain plots for their wives to cultivate and concern themselves with problems of irrigation. In short, they must undertake many of the economic responsibilities of elders—from which they were traditionally free—without enjoying all the privileges or the status of that grade. For instance, they are still forbidden to drink beer. Moreover, they are still required to join with their age-mates to perform the prescribed ritual and dancing at village festivals. A married *motana* attempts to act out two different roles which are not yet integrated and are conflicting at some points. (2) The second major change concerns the activities of the junior *batana*. By present custom, after his initiation a young man normally spends about two years in the village living the traditional life of a warrior. Then he may leave his homeland and go out into the world to earn money for a period of from two to four years. This is now done by the majority of the *batana* of Kheri, Ebwe, and Soyetu, but it is said that the custom is only starting at Rokhari and Kura and that most of the *batana* from those villages stay at home. Little information was obtained from Orokhata. As might be expected from their intensive apprenticeship in goat raising, the Sonjo *batana* have specialized in goat trading. Young Sonjo traders now may be seen at some of the government livestock auctions in central and northern Tanganyika buying goats and driving them to markets at Arusha or other centres of population. Since this study has the primary aim of presenting the traditional social system of the Sonjo, these recent changes and the complex social conflicts which they have brought in their train will not be further discussed here.

Age-sets in later life

With the second initiation ceremony following their own, and after serving fourteen years as warriors, the men of an age-set are promoted to the grade of 'elders'. Thereafter their age-set loses most of its formal structure and functions. It continues to exist on the level of an informal alumni association, supported largely by the sentiment engendered by the past association of members. Since the members are mostly neighbours in the village or ward anyway, there is no need for special reunions. Men who visit different villages normally look to their age-mates for hospitality. Except for this mutual obligation of hospitality, the only strict rule enjoined on members of the same age-set prohibits them from marrying each other's daughters. Sisters of age-mates, however, may be married freely.

Upon becoming an elder a man finds himself involved in irrigation problems for the first time in his life. In seeking for rights to irrigation water he is jostled into position in the class structure of the village. The age-grade system no longer directly affects him, for the grade of elder is not formally subdivided into smaller age divisions.

FUNCTIONAL INTERPRETATION

The Sonjo age-grade system could be interpreted in different ways depending on the type of problem to be solved. Thus the circumcision and initiation ceremonies could be considered as *rites de passage*, in the sense that Van Gennep made familiar to anthropology, and analysed in terms of social psychology and symbolism. The age-grades could also be interpreted as part of

the indigenous system of education. These approaches will not
be further explored here, as they do not materially contribute
to the solution of the problems with which we are primarily
concerned in this study: namely, the ecological adaptation of
the society and its social structure. The question we should ask
is: What are the functions of the age-grade system which are
relevant to these problems?

In considering the social functions of institutions, it is useful
to distinguish between *manifest* and *latent* functions, a distinction
defined by Merton (1949:61) as 'between conscious motivations
for social behaviour and its objective consequences'. Manifest
functions often apply only in a particular situation and it is
more difficult to generalize about them. Perhaps for this reason,
social scientists have tended to be concerned mostly with latent
functions. This has been the case in most studies of age systems.
Thus Prins (1953 : 124) in a comparative study of East African
age-grades interprets their latent function as a determinant of
status: '. . . in our East African societies the status system is
essentially an age-class system, and based on social age'. This is
only in small part true of the Sonjo, for as we shall see later,
after a man has left the military age-grades behind him he
becomes involved in a status system based on property and
irrigation rights in which age-grades play no part. In another,
more general, study of age-grades, Eisenstadt (1956 : 50) pro-
poses a different latent function. 'Their function is to extend
the solidarity of the kinship system to the whole social system
through emphasis on diffuse age-group membership.' Again,
this function is not very apparent among the Sonjo. If the
solidarity of the Sonjo is more broadly based than in the case of
their neighbours—if their society is more 'universalistic', to use
Eisenstadt's term—the reason for this is to be found elsewhere
than in the age-grade system.

The manifest function of Sonjo age-grades, as any thoughtful Sonjo would explain, is to provide a military force to protect
the villages against attack by their enemies the Masai. It is
certain that similar functions are served by the age-grade
systems of many other African societies, but this tends to be
overlooked in comparative studies, perhaps because it is so
obvious. After the arrival of the Masai, if not before, the Sonjo
had urgent need for a disciplined, trained defensive force if

they were to survive and maintain their delicately balanced ecological adjustment to the environment. They solved this problem by a system of universal conscription of the young men of warrior age. In effect, they established a permanent standing army. This had many objective consequences—that is, the age-grades had latent functions—but these could not be predicted on the basis of any general theory of age-grades that has been proposed. They stem from the concrete historical and ecological conditions in which Sonjo society developed.

In terms of exploitative manpower, the age-grade system served a negative function. It deprived the society of a large amount of potential labour, tied up in the warrior age-sets, which might otherwise have been applied in productive activities: for the army provided full-time occupation for young adult men, and they had to be provisioned by the rest of the society. A sizeable military force in any society, besides protecting the society against foreign enemies, is an instrument of political power within the society. The political rulers must control the army and retain its loyalty. The rulers of a Sonjo village do maintain this control and loyalty; the warriors serve them as a police force to enforce their orders if need be, though occasions where this function is exercised seldom arise. In chapter VIII we shall examine more closely the structure of social control and political power in a Sonjo village and note the role of the age-sets in this structure.

Chapter VII

RELIGION

IN this chapter I shall be describing myths, ritual, and sacred places and objects, and discussing the relations of these categories to social institutions. I shall also speak of religious 'beliefs', and to that term I attach a special anthropological meaning. Religious belief, in this sense, does not have the connotation of assured knowledge of ascertained or probable facts. Rather it connotes an appreciation of the significance of accepted myths, or of certain elements or propositions in those myths. This appreciation evokes certain prescribed actions or attitudes which may be described as 'ritual'. In an unsophisticated society such as the Sonjo, the question of the matter-of-fact or historical truth of the myths does not arise. Even those few Sonjo, Lutheran converts, who challenge the myths, argue not that they are untrue but that they are irrelevant; from the newly acquired Christian viewpoint, the myths lose their significance. For 'believers' the significance of each myth, or mythical elements, is appreciated in its ritual context. In the non-ritual context of ordinary life (conditions under which anthropologists normally record myths) the details of the myths do not arouse much interest. Sonjo informants are not disturbed when inconsistencies or contradictions in the myths are pointed out, nor do they attempt to explain or justify them. The validity of the myth lies in the ritual action which they know it will evoke at the proper time and place. Myth and ritual mutually support one another and they unfold together as the seasons pass by in the yearly cycle. When I abstract from this complex of myth and ritual certain important points and call them beliefs, I use the word 'belief' in this special sense.

Sonjo beliefs are mainly concerned with a supernatural being called Khambageu, with his history, his nature, and his relations with the Sonjo. Khambageu first appeared in the world in an unusual way; he performed miracles and ushered in a golden age for the Sonjo; upon his death he ascended into the sky and became identified with God; he now dwells in the sun or the summit of Oldonyo Lengai Mountain or in both places; he is concerned with the welfare of the Sonjo and takes note of sacrifices and prayers; once a year he visits each of the villages and is then honoured with a festival; during his stay on earth he originated certain customs, which have been followed ever since without change; he also issued commands which should be obeyed; certain places and objects associated with his life on earth remain sacred and are treated as such; at the end of the world he will save all faithful Sonjo, though other peoples may be destroyed.

MYTHOLOGY

The myths are not strictly coherent or consistent. A central myth relating the principal events in the life of Khambageu appears to be fairly well standardized, though some of the details differ in versions told at different villages. Each village has special myths telling of the doings of Khambageu at that village. The special myths of one village are not usually known by, or of interest to, the other villages. A number of culture traits are believed to have been created or originated by Khambageu. In some cases these beliefs are based on detailed myths of origin; in other cases there is nothing more than the assertion that Khambageu commanded that this be done. A few of the myths are concerned with happenings in the world before the advent of Khambageu. A concise account of the principal myths follows.

Creation myth

Naka, a god, and his sister Nebele, a goddess, were the first beings to appear in the world. They were both creators and vied with one another in creating. Nebele created everything except man. Thereupon Naka became jealous; he told her that she was only a woman and therefore his property, and he proceeded to brand her like a goat. Nebele was angry at this and ran away to another world. She has not been seen since. Naka then created a man and a woman, and their children were the founders of all the tribes of the world. Naka gave each tribe one gift, whatever they asked for. The Sonjo asked for and received the digging-stick.

At Soyetu the first Sonjo, who was given the digging-stick, is said to have been a man named Mwegumune who later founded the village of Soyetu.

The realm of the dead

The Sonjo, like other African peoples, believe in life after death, but their ideas about the ghosts of the dead and the conditions of their existence are characteristically vague. I only discovered this one myth dealing with the realm of the dead. As we shall see, it is related to some important customs with regard to divorce and remarriage.

In the early days of the Sonjo, the ghosts of the dead could return to this world for visits if they so wished. One woman had four daughters who helped her cultivate her fields. The daughters all died suddenly. After that the woman was not able to keep her fields cultivated properly. She became poverty-stricken and her husband left her. One morning she was astonished to find her fields freshly and thoroughly cultivated. She returned to the house and there found her four daughters grinding flour and doing the housework. They promised to do all her work for her but forbade her to talk to them or touch them or to tell anyone else about them. After that her affairs prospered so well that the neighbours started talking about her and her husband decided to return to her. The husband was curious and suspicious about his wife's prosperity. He hid himself in the house one morning, and when the daughters arrived he seized one of them, the other three running away. He found that his daughter had no bones in her body but was all soft flesh. She reproved him for having touched her. Never again, she said, would the dead come to visit the living. Before leaving him she explained about marriage customs among the dead and commanded that the living should behave in accordance with these customs. When a man dies, she said, his ghost waits in the other world for his widow, who joins him there after her death, and the same is true of a fiancé who dies before his marriage. For that reason a widow can never be the full wife of another man. Although she is normally inherited by her husband's brother and expected to live intimately with him, she is not really his proper wife. If the dead husband's heir wishes to divorce her and sell her to another man, he can demand only

H

thirty goats for her, which is considerably less than her normal bride-price; for the new husband only acquires temporal rights over her in this world and cannot claim her as an eternal wife.

The rules governing divorce and remarriage, which were discussed in chapter v, are in agreement with this myth and find in it a sanction which reinforces their validity.

The life of Khambageu

The myth to be presented here is based on a text dictated by Simon Ndula and written in Swahili by a government court clerk, Gabriel Mavalla. It was translated, edited, and published by H. A. Fosbrooke (1955 : 38–42). I have added a few important points from other sources. This myth constitutes the core of Sonjo mythology and is accepted at all villages with only minor variations. According to the text, Khambageu came into the world 'automatically and not through the natural way, i.e. birth. That is to say he had neither father nor mother.' I encountered some disagreement with this statement: one elder said that Khambageu's father was known to the ancient Sonjo, and that Khambageu was formerly believed to have been born miraculously from his father's swollen leg. However, it seems now to be generally accepted that Khambageu appeared in the world without parents as stated in the text.

Khambageu first appeared at a village called Tinaga (no longer in existence; see chapter i) in a state of poverty. He worked at the humble task of guarding crops against birds. In time he acquired a herd of five goats. On several occasions he refused to do his share of work on the irrigation furrows. Each time he was fined several goats, but in spite of this he remained in possession of five goats, which caused the people to be suspicious and envious of him. Because of his continued refusal to share in communal work, the elders of the village sentenced him to death. On the day set for his death Khambageu miraculously cured an old woman of her blindness and sent her to Soyetu to prepare that village as his sanctuary. When the execution party arrived at his hut he first went into a convulsive seizure; then he escapes from the hut by a trick. Khambageu was pursued all the way to Soyetu and had several adventures and close escapes *en route*. Arriving at Soyetu well ahead of his enemies he was cordially received by the villagers and offered sanctuary. When the Tinaga party arrived they demanded that Khambageu be turned over to them and threatened to seize him by force. At this tense moment Khambageu asked for some guinea-fowl feathers, which he threw at his pursuers. The feathers burst into flame and wounded many of the Tinaga men. The others retreated in terror and left the country of the Sonjo, migrating to Ikoma where they founded the Ikoma tribe. They are supposed to have suddenly lost their ability to speak and understand the Sonjo language. Soon after this the village of Tinaga suffered famine and pestilence, and the remaining inhabitants abandoned the village and moved to Keri where they formed the Watinaga clan.

Khambageu then settled down to a position of honour at Soyetu. Every day he performed miracles. He cured all sicknesses, ensured good crops, and even resurrected the dead. He took care of children and fed them while their mothers worked in the fields, and he settled all disputes that were brought before him. This happy state of affairs lasted many years. Khambageu married a wife who bore him many children. He grew tired of having so many children and turned them all into stones except for two sons, one of whom was later banished. The stones were dispersed through the country and to each one was attached the spirit of the child whom it represented. Khambageu was very fond of the remaining son, named Aka, and lived with him for many years. One day while his father was sleeping Aka called the people of the village together to bid them farewell, and then flew away like a bird. Khambageu was deeply grieved upon hearing this news. About this time the people started making excessive demands on Khambageu, and they would even abuse him when he was too tired to serve them.

Finally Khambageu decided to leave Soyetu and move to Rokhari. The people tried in vain to prevent him, and after he had left they sent delegations to persuade or force him to return. He deceitfully promised to return to Soyetu in order to get rid of the delegation. He then made a prolonged visit to Belwa, the village of his origin. When he returned to Rokhari he was an old man and very tired. He told the people that he would soon die and directed that his body be laid on a certain rock to dry in the sun, or else that it be taken to Soyetu for burial. Then he retired to his hut and died. Instead of obeying his request, the

people of Rokhari buried him in their own village. The Soyetu
elders were angry when they heard about this and came to
disinter the body. When the grave was opened it was found to
be empty except for the sandals in which Khambageu had been
buried. It transpired that some of the people had seen him rise
from the grave and fly up to the sun. Khambageu had once
said: 'Soyetu is my feet; Rokhari is my head.' The people of
the two villages now fully recognized him as God. A temple was
built at the site of his grave in Rokhari, and the people of
Soyetu became the guardians of the memory of the golden age
of Sonjo.

A psychological interpretation

The Fosbrooke text of the Khambageu myth has been
analysed by E. Simenauer (1955) from the viewpoint of psycho-
analytical theory. This myth, he concludes, is diagnostic of a
narcissistic trait in Sonjo personality. His argument is not
always easy to follow. Although he clearly regards the story as
a myth, and discusses the 'dynamics of myth-creating' among
the Sonjo, at times he treats the story as if it were a factual
account of Khambageu as a historical person. Khambageu
himself is diagnosed as a Narciss, and therefore he was rejected
by the people of Tinaga among whom 'narcissistic characteristics were strikingly absent'. However, he appealed so strongly to
the narcissism of the other Sonjo that they made him their God.

This is a very interesting commentary on the myth and on
Sonjo psychology generally, but as Simenauer's interpretation
does not directly bear on the structural problems which concerns
us in this book, I shall not further discuss it here.

Village origins

The myth just related appears to be accepted by all Sonjo
and may be taken to represent the official scripture of the tribe.
However, each village has a complex of local myths, some of
which are mutually contradictory. Thus every village claims
to have been founded by Khambageu, this despite the statements in the central myth that the villages were already in
existence when Khambageu first visited them. The origin myths
of three of the villages will be briefly summarized here.

The first man to arrive at the site of Soyetu was named Mwegumune. He was a farmer and came from Belwa, bringing a digging-stick with him. He took possession of the only spring and started to cultivate crops, but he had no fire to cook food with. The second man to arrive was Msarunda, a hunter, who came with a bow and arrow and a fire drill. Mwegumune was envious of Msarunda's fire and Msarunda was envious of Mwegumune's water. Khambageu, who was at Belwa, perceived this unsatisfactory situation and sent Msarunda's sister Nkaribieri to Soyetu with two magical stones. While passing near Rokhari she accidentally dropped one of the stones and at that spot a spring gushed forth. The villagers were delighted because previously they had had no spring. She continued her journey and brought the other stone to her brother at Soyetu. The next morning, as she had been directed by Khambageu, she took the stone to Mwegaro hill and dropped it. Immediately a large spring started to flow from the spot. Nkaribieri claimed the water from this spring for herself as she had created it. Her brother was angry at this for he coveted the water, and he killed her on the spot with his spear. Her blood stained the stones at the spring, and they remain red to this day. Mwegumune and Msarunda then agreed to combine the water from their two springs into a single furrow that could be used to irrigate the valley. They both obtained wives, other people came to join them, and soon the village was fully inhabited. Two of the Soyetu clans (and wards), Egumune and Sarunda, bear the names of the two founders.

The twin villages of Kheri and Ebwe share a common myth of origin. This story begins at a place called Mageri which is said to have been located at Nguruman north of Lake Natron. It was inhabited by the forerunners of the Sonjo. Famine and pestilence forced most of the people to migrate to a place called Moholo which is located on the plain roughly midway between the present Sonjo villages. These people took on the name Batemi, which has remained the name by which the Sonjo call themselves. The land at Moholo was fertile but there was no water for irrigation. Successive groups of Batemi moved away to sites with irrigation water until all the villages were founded except Kheri and Ebwe. Finally the remaining people were

driven from Moholo by drought, and under the leadership of
Kimasaija they migrated to the site of the twin villages. There
they met another group who had just come from Mageri and
were led by Khambageu. The two parties agreed to found a new
village, and at first they lived together peacefully. Soon they
started quarrelling about irrigation water, which was supplied
by a single small stream, inadequate for their needs. Khambageu
then slaughtered a goat at each of a number of places at the foot
of the escarpment, and at each place a spring gushed forth,
thus supplying the village with sufficient water for irrigation.
Kimasaija's group then demanded control of all irrigation
water. The other group made a counterclaim to the water, and
Khambageu challenged Kimasaija to a duel to settle the matter.
Kimasaija, however, mindful of Khambageu's miracles, refused.
In the end the village was divided into two separate villages,
each with its own water supply and block of cultivated fields.
Since the villages were adjacent, they shared a common
defensive palisade, but each village had its own gateway. When
these arrangements were completed Khambageu disappeared
from the scene.

At both Ebwe and Kheri there are temples which are
believed to be houses once used by Khambageu and kept in
repair constantly since that time. These houses were not,
however, built at the time the villages were founded as described in the last myth. They are supposed to have been built
for Khambageu when he visited the villages for the first time on
his journey from Soyetu to Rokhari as recounted in the central
myth. The obvious discrepancy in chronology between these
two myths does not in the least disturb the people when it is
pointed out to them. The fact that these myths are in accordance with present ritual attitudes and behaviour outweighs
their lack of chronological consistency as narrative.

Miscellaneous myths of origin

The miraculous creation of springs at three of the villages
was described in the mythical accounts of the origins of the
villages. It is further asserted that Khambageu placed each
spring in the ritual safekeeping of a clan. This event is not
integrated with any narrative, but appears to be an *ad hoc*
explanation of the fact that certain clans perform ritual at

certain springs. Many of the sacred places and objects in the villages are similarly explained by isolated and fragmentary myths which simply state that Khambageu once sat on this rock, flew to the top of that tree, or commanded that a shrine be built at a certain place, without reference to any of the longer myths. In giving these brief explanations informants often imply that more details were formerly known about the circumstances in which these places and objects were given their sacred character.

Many of the traditional culture traits of the Sonjo are implicitly believed to have been initiated or in some way sanctioned by Khambageu. These beliefs are explicitly stated when the people become aware that a trait is in danger of being eliminated or replaced by a new trait. One of the first traits to be thus threatened with change was the traditional skin garments. The wearing of cloths and blankets is still resented by many of the elders, and up to about 1953 it was totally prohibited in the temple village of Rokhari. Prior to that time the schoolboys were required to change from cloths to skins before entering the village on their return from school. At present skin garments must be worn at all ritual occasions, but the belief is growing that Khambageu has consented to the wearing of cloths and blankets in ordinary secular life.

The digging-stick is more firmly rooted in sacred myth, and up to now the people have resolutely refused to replace it as a cultivating tool with the obviously more efficient hoe. It is believed to be a unique gift from God to the Sonjo as stated in the creation myth cited above, and this belief is reinforced by several other myths. Rather inconsistently iron hoes are now widely used by the men for cleaning and repairing the main irrigation furrows; however, in working on the small ditches around their plots, the men use only digging-sticks.

Although the Sonjo traditionally kept no cattle, they are immensely interested in the subject. They vigorously deny the suggestion that they were prevented from keeping cattle by the Masai, who would doubtless have raided and plundered them of any cattle they possessed. Instead they cite a divine injunction against cattle-raising as an explanation for their traditional lack of cattle. I collected three different myths on this theme, one of which follows.

One day as Khambageu wandered in the forest, disguised as a homeless old man, he met two Sonjo girls carrying home water and asked them for a drink. They refused him, saying that he stank and was not fit to drink from their father's gourd. He then performed magic and turned the girls into logs and their gourds into monkeys. A third girl passed by with a gourd of water, and when Khambageu asked her for a drink she gladly gave it to him. She also perceived what had happened to the two girls and begged to have them restored to their proper forms, which was done for her. Khambageu then asked the third girl for a meal and walked home with her. Her family was poor and they had only a bone for food. Khambageu told them to boil it, but there was no water in the house. He pulled up the centre pole of the house and water flowed out of the ground; when the water gourds had been filled, he replaced the centre pole. After the bone was boiled he asked for a stick to divide the 'meat' with. The girl was surprised, but she gave him a stick and he miraculously dished up big helpings of meat all round. Before going to bed Khambageu told the people not to get up in the night if they heard anything unusual. In the night a herd of cattle came down from the sky with a loud noise of lowing and pounding of hoofs. The girl got up and gave a cry of joy when she looked through the door and saw the cattle. In the morning the people went out and milked the cows. They started quarrelling about how to divide the cattle. Because of this show of disobedience and greed, Khambageu turned the cattle into forest animals and told the people that thereafter they could never keep cattle.

Solar myths

The sun plays an important role in Sonjo religion, though it is overshadowed by the dominant figure of Khambageu. The evidence of mythology suggests that the sun formerly occupied a more central position in the religion. In two versions of the basic biographical myth of Khambageu there are different endings. In one version Khambageu is said to have ascended to the summit of Oldonyo Lengai after his resurrection from the grave. The other one, supposedly based on eye-witness evidence, states that Khambageu flew straight up to the sun. One of the other of these places, or even both of them, are asserted to be his present abode, depending on the mythological context of the conversation. Khambageu not only inhabits the sun but is actually identified with it, and he is also called Riob, 'the sun'. Evidently the Sonjo originally recognized an impersonal sun-god Riob, and with the development of their present cult the culture hero Khambageu came to be identified with Riob through a process of syncretism. The word *mugwe* is a generic term for God and is also used in the plural form—*bagwe*. It is applied to Khambageu and Riob and sometimes to Khambageu's son Aka. In his role as sun-god, Khambageu-Riob is thought to rule the heavens. The stars are conceived of as his children. There exist some stellar myths based on the rudimentary astronomy of the Sonjo, but these were not well known by my informants.

The sun also figures in a myth which explains the origin of the priesthood. A man was once bathing in a stream, so the myth goes, and had laid his skin cloak carefully on the bank. Suddenly the sun swooped down on him from the sky and temporarily blinded him. When he regained his vision he saw a large white stone lying on his clothes glittering like a diamond. He took the stone home and showed it to the astonished people. He kept the stone for a number of days. At night it would emit light like a star. One night he was told in a dream that he had been appointed by God to perform sacrifices for the Sonjo, and when he awoke the stone had disappeared. Thereafter he supervised sacrifices to God, and when he died his sons inherited the office of priest.

Another short sun myth was recorded, after I had left the Sonjo, by a District Officer, Mr. F. G. Finch (1957). A virgin was bathing in a stream one day when her comrades saw a sunbeam come from the sky and strike her. The girl became pregnant and gave birth to a child. The child was known as a child of the sun.

Eschatalogical myths

The Sonjo view of the future is decidedly apocalyptic and contrasts sharply with the usual outlook of African societies, in which the future is regarded with a placid expectation that oncoming generations will continue indefinitely to follow the customs of their ancestors. The Sonjo do not have millennial expectations that conditions in this world will be improved in

the future. Instead they believe that the world will come to an
end at some unknown date in the future, and they have fairly
definite ideas about the signs that will precede this catastrophe
and the sequence of events which will follow.

There will come a time when warfare and quarrelling increase throughout the world. One day the sun will be progressively obscured by the successive appearances of a great
flock of birds, a swarm of bees, and a cloud of dust. Then two
suns will arise from the horizon, one in the east and one in the
west. This means that the end of the world is imminent.
Khambageu has warned the people that at that time they
should lay in a supply of water and retire to their huts, putting
out all fires and sitting in the dark. When the two suns meet at
the top of the sky the world will rapidly shrink and come to an
end. Khambageu will then appear and save all Sonjo who are
properly marked with the *ntemi* scar under the left breast.
According to a version of the myth recorded by Finch (1957),
Khambageu will send his son Aka to save the Sonjo at the end
of the world. The Sonjo believe that the dead as well as the
living will somehow be saved, but they are unable to explain
coherently how this will be accomplished. In this respect the
prospective myths of the Sonjo resemble popular Christian
beliefs in which there is uncertainty as to the nature and
sequence of the last events—resurrection, judgement, and so
forth.

RITUAL

The three principal festivals of the Sonjo, all of which are
synchronized with the agricultural cycle, will be discussed here,
and also some of the special rites which are not performed
according to a seasonal schedule. The Sonjo attitude to sacred
places and objects, both actual and mythological, is essentially
ritual in nature and will also be discussed briefly. On the other
hand, some of the *rites de passage*—specifically the rites and
ceremonies connected with birth, initiation, marriage, and
death—are dealt with elsewhere in the book and will not be
considered here. These rites are undoubtedly a part of Sonjo
religion, but they serve special social functions and are only
loosely integrated with the main cult; further analysis of them
would contribute little to the understanding of this cult.

Harvest festival

A festival called Mbarimbari (the name referring to the green clay used for decorating the bodies of the dancers) is celebrated in each village after the harvest has been gathered. At Orokhata and Soyetu the Mbarimbari festival takes place in August after the *magare* crops have been harvested. At the other four villages the Mbarimbari is celebrated after the harvesting of the *hura* crops in April. I was able to observe the entire festival at Soyetu. According to informants the same programme of events that was witnessed at the Soyetu festival is also followed at the other villages. The festival lasts for five days and several days more are spent in preparations; thus the ordinary work of the village comes to a standstill for a week or so.

The festival at Soyetu started with a procession of people who walked to Rokhari bearing offerings to the temple of Khambageu. This village delegation is supposed to consist of eight men and eight women. The delegates—both men and women—must meet with strict qualifications. They must be in good health and free of any skin lesion. They must come from families in which there has never been a murderer. And—most important of all—they must be in a tranquil benevolent frame of mind. If a person had recently been involved in any kind of violence or aggressive action he would be automatically disqualified as a delegate. If a person harbours feelings of envy or ill will he is expected to disqualify himself and refuse to be a delegate. Should an unqualified person nevertheless join the delegation, it is believed that an omen would be observed before the party reached Rokhari, warning them to turn back and purge their number of unqualified members. As offerings, the delegation brings eight goats (which are supplied by the *wakiama* and must be of a certain size and colour), four large gourds of honey beer, and four bags of grain. The women carried the beer and grain while the men drove the goats. The party left Soyetu about 10 a.m. and arrived at Rokhari in mid-afternoon. The other villages follow a similar programme in celebrating their festivals, though the pilgrimage to Rokhari will be longer or shorter accordingly as the distances between villages differ.

Soon after the party arrives at Rokhari two of the goats are killed and their stomachs and livers are examined for omens by priests. If the omens are favourable the goats are cut up for cooking; bracelets and rings are cut from the skin of the goats' foreheads and worn ritually by the men. But if the omens are unfavourable, the carcass of the goat is given to the elders of Rokhari, who must then supply a suitable live goat in its place. The visiting delegation is only permitted to eat cold food during its stay. Therefore the priests accept the offerings of grain immediately and their wives start grinding flour and cooking food for the visitors so that it will be cool in time for the evening meal. The remaining six goats are turned over to the priests, who accept them on behalf of Khambageu. The visitors spend the whole night in the temple precincts with the priests, singing, dancing, and drinking beer. A small calabash of beer is placed in each of the three temples. Later these are examined by the elders who expect to find that some of the beer has been taken by Khambageu as a sign that the offering is accepted and that the festival may proceed. The next day the delegation returns to its home village to announce that the dancing and cere- monies may start on the following day.

The festivities in the village consist mainly in a programme of dancing and singing that goes on for four days. The *batana* are the chief performers. About a week before the start of the festival the *batana*, both the junior and senior sets, ask for goats from their fathers or other senior relatives. They then retire to camps in the forest and begin feasting on the goats. Many of them stay in the camps until the first morning of the festival, feasting and gathering strength for the dancing to come. For the last several days they prepare infusions of various barks, which are mixed with meat broth and drunk freely. The camps are organized in a military way, with sentries posted at the approaches and regular patrols sent out to scout the neighbour- hood, because even today there is always danger of a raid by a band of Masai *moran* who would try to plunder the goats. By the time the village festival is due to begin the *batana* are well nourished and have worked themselves up to a pitch of excite- ment.

At dawn on the first day of the festival the *batana* assemble near the principal spring, where they are met by several elders who have the special task of supervising them. First the elders make a mystical mark on the face of each *motan* with the green-ish-white clay (*mbarimbari*) which is used throughout the festival. These marks are then washed off and the *batana* decorate their own bodies with the clay, the designs differing for the junior and senior grades. The decorations and costumes of the two age-sets differ in other respects as well. The senior warriors wear their hair long in carefully braided plaits that fall to the shoulders. Some of them braid pieces of black yarn into their hair to increase its length, a custom which they admit was borrowed from the Masai. The junior *batana* had relatively short hair in 1955, as it was less than a year since they had been shaved at initiation. In succeeding gears their hair would be worn longer and longer. The senior *batana* used a mixture of red ochre and fat for decorating their bodies above the waist. The juniors did not do this, but they wore a distinctive headdress of ostrich feathers similar to those worn by Masai *moran*. Every *motana* wore an anklet of white feathers and a special bracelet of buffalo horn, and carried a long wand with a tuft of white feathers at the tip. A girdle of beads was worn round the waist; to this was attached a penis guard of cloth or leather, which failed, however, adequately to conceal that organ. In addition to the wand, most of the men carried a club, and a bouquet of green leaves was tucked under one arm.

While the warriors were painting themselves and adjusting their ornaments, the supervising elders conferred with the leaders of the different companies about the programme to be followed in the dancing. The men were also reminded of the rules governing behaviour during the festival: there was to be no fighting, and while dancing the warriors were supposed to give no recognition or attention to the spectators. In the meanwhile the people of the village had been gathering just outside the village gate, which was about 300 yards from the grove that served as headquarters for the *batana*. At nine o'clock the dancers came out in single file and trotted once in a large circle around the large open space before the gateway. After that for about two hours they came out in small groups of two, four, or eight warriors and performed various special dances, mostly in the area outside the gate, but sometimes running through the main paths of the village. After that, all the senior *batana* joined together for some dances, and the juniors did likewise. Finally the whole group of about sixty warriors formed in one body and performed a dance accompanied by energetic singing. By then a dense cloud of dust all but obscured the scene. At a given signal the warriors formed in a double file and danced through the gate and up the steep path to the central plaza of the village, which was already surrounded by spectators. Here they drew up in two ranks and performed a competitive dance called *gikhoji* in which the object was to jump as high as possible without perceptibly bending the knees. The Sonjo claim to surpass the Masai in this jumping dance. It was now two o'clock in the afternoon and they had been dancing in the hot sun for five hours. Two of the junior warriors had seizures in which they rolled on the ground, frothed at the mouth, and had some clonic movements of their limbs. This happens every year, I was told, on the first and second day of the festival; usually two warriors are affected at a time. These seizures are partly the result of the stimulating herbs which are taken in the camps and partly of excitement and the expectation of having such a seizure. The Masai are said to have the same kind of convulsive seizures at their *manyatta* feasts of meat. The dancing came to an end shortly after this episode.

Late in the afternoon a few *batana* gathered at the plaza and started a slow shuffling dance. They were joined by other *batana* and also by the girls of the village. This dancing was informal and anyone in the village could take part in it. The rhythm was beat out on cymbals which were simply hoe blades that had been furnished by the government some years before, but which had never been put to use as agricultural implements. These cymbals are only used for the Mbarimbari festival. The traditional musical instrument for this dancing, before it was replaced by the hoes, was a wooden clapper which is no longer in existence. The elders of the village celebrate the festival by drinking as much honey beer as they can obtain. In the evening a number of them joined the dancers at the plaza. They formed a circle of their own and performed some old-boy dances which were caricatures of the dances of the younger people. The dancing broke up before midnight, but at other times it may go on till dawn. The *batana* returned to their camps to eat more meat and drink herb tea.

On the second day the *batana* formed ranks at the plaza

shortly before noon and then danced through the village for an hour or so, ending up with the vigorous *gikhoji* dance. In the heat of the afternoon everyone rested, and in the evening there was informal dancing by the whole village. For the last two days the dancing was mostly informal. The *batana* began to appear exhausted; their goat meat was finished and the stimulating effect of the herbal drugs was wearing off. The elders too had finished their beer and began to look bleary-eyed and cross.

Although the Mbarimbari festival is regarded as essentially religious, once the delegation has returned from the temple at Rokhari, it is a period of licence: drunkenness is permitted of the elders, and the *batana* go virtually naked in contrast to the everyday rules of behaviour which are strict in requiring them to be decently clad. It would seem that sexual irregularities might easily occur during the unsettled period of the festival, but definite information on this point is lacking. There is a special rule that forbids quarrelling in the village or the beating of wives and children for ten days after the festival; this is meant to prevent men from acting rashly while suffering from the irritability and jangled nerves of their hangovers.

The Mase festival

The second Sonjo festival is altogether different in character from the Mbarimbari festival. The general atmosphere is one of sobriety and piety rather than of excitement and drunkenness. The Mase[1] festival is celebrated for four or five days at each village. The whole cycle lasts about six weeks, starting in late October and extending into December. During this period all members of the tribe are supposed to be on good behaviour and quarrelling and fighting is forbidden. Within the village that is actually celebrating, the rules of behaviour are very strict. Individuals must not only refrain from unseemly overt acts, such as scolding, laughing, or shouting, but they must also banish all thoughts or feelings of anger, hate, resentment, greed, envy, and the like, all of which are regarded as impious. Honey beer is drunk by the elders but only in moderation and in a ritualistic manner as a symbol of hospitality; for there is much

---

[1] The significance of the name Mase was not known to my informants and the derivation of the word was not determined.

visiting between villages at this time, and all visiting elders must be given a drink of beer by the leaders of the host village.

The Mase festival starts after the *hura* crops have been planted and the young seedlings have begun to grow. The dry season is well advanced, and for the next few months the crops will require constant irrigation. There is no special anxiety about water at this time—for the springs have never been known to fail—but the sharp contrast between the fresh green of the irrigated fields and the prevailing whiteness of the desiccated countryside impresses everyone with the vital importance of irrigation water. Khambageu, who is believed to dwell on the summit of Oldonyo Lengai, comes at this time to visit each Sonjo village in turn, where he receives offerings, observes ritual, listens to petitions, prayers, and protestations of good behaviour, and grants blessings to individuals and to the village as a whole.

The festival is celebrated first at Orokhata and then at the other villages in a set order, ending at Soyetu. The day for starting the cycle is no doubt decided upon by the *wenamiji* and the priests, and each village knows roughly when its own festival will start. But in theory Khambageu himself sets the date for each festival by arriving in the village and making his presence known in a loud 'voice'. It is a very important tenet of Sonjo belief that Khambageu is present in the villages at this time in a form that is material to the extent that he is capable of making a sound like the blast of a horn. My informants took it amiss when I expressed cynical doubts as to the source of the horn blast that they called the voice of Khambageu. Even the Lutherans, who were generally contemptuous of their native religion, equating Khambageu with the Devil, for example, rather than with God, refused to deny that the sound of the horn was indeed the voice of Khambageu. In the daytime the 'voice' generally comes from the small thatched shelter in the *khoseri*—the closed in, sacred end of the village plaza. At night it may come from other points in the village or from the surrounding forest. It can be heard at irregular intervals night and day throughout the four days of the festival.

Skin garments are worn by everyone in the village except for the uninitiated boys—the *vijori*—most of whom wear their customary tattered cloths. Elders, women, and girls wear their best skin cloaks; the *batana* wear special garments of soft, chamois-like leather which are worn as skirts and fall below their knees. Any indecent exposure is strictly forbidden. The *batana* wear a special ornament consisting of a wicker hoop strapped to the upper left arm in such a way that the curved end projects above the shoulder, but they do not paint their bodies or carry anything in their hands. At the *khoseri* end of the plaza a percussion instrument, called a *kiripelo*, is erected consisting of a bundle of dry sticks, the sticks being about an inch thick and ten feet long and the whole bundle measuring about a foot in diameter. This is mounted on a stand and beaten during the dancing by an elder with a stout billet of wood in each hand. Sometimes two or three elders beat the *kiripelo* at the same time, producing a clacking thud which goes on most of the time from mid-morning till midnight.

The daily programme during the festival starts before dawn: the whole population of the village gathers at the plaza; some of the *wenamiji* go to the various springs to make sacrifices; other *wenamiji* together with the village priests perform a rite at the guardhouse in which a fire is kindled with wood from the sacred grove adjoining the gateway—the *senge ya kijome* ('forest of the gate'). When the sun appears on the horizon the assembled people sing a hymn, and then the crowd breaks up to return to their houses. During the Mase festival the offerings of goats to Khambageu are made by individuals, who deliver their goats to the village temples where they are received by priests. This is done in the early morning. At about ten o'clock the sound of the horn summons the *batana* to the plaza where they form a circle and start dancing and singing. This goes on till one o'clock, then there is a break until five o'clock when dancing is resumed and continues till midnight. The dancing is divided into episodes lasting about twenty minutes. The circle of dancers starts at the open end of the plaza and revolves in a counterclockwise direction, at the same time moving slowly towards the *khoseri*. The dancers intertwine their arms behind their backs and execute a slow rhythmic movement with their hips, shoulders, and necks, taking very small steps with their feet. They sing in two-part harmony humming without articulating words. They are accompanied most of the time by the beating of the *kiripelo*. Occasionally when the dancers seem

I

to be flagging several of the elders will freshen the rhythm by exceptionally vigorous beating of the sticks. When the circle of dancers reaches the *khoseri* that episode of the dance is ended.

Between episodes the *batana* and elders group themselves around the *khoseri*; the other people of the village are standing or sitting around the edge of the plaza. Then an elder starts chanting a petition to Khambageu. The chant always begins with a formal invocation: *Aja Riob, aja Khambageu, turaseri otu-toli ndipa ja Belwa* ('Father Riob, Father Khambageu, bless us and open for us the sluices of Belwa'). He then goes on to present petitions to Khambageu for individuals who have brought offerings to the temple, specifying what the offering consists of, stating that the individual has led a blameless life during the last year, and beseeching God for the blessings that the individual specially desires—usually a child, good crops, fertility of his goats, or recovery from a sickness in the family. Sometimes the chant is devoted wholly to a request for communal blessings, either general or specific. The chanter is never a priest and need not be a *mwenamiji*; any elder with a strong voice and having a good record of behaviour is eligible for the office, which changes hands frequently during the festival. The chant is punctuated at intervals by the sound of the horn, which is interpreted as indicating the assent of Khambageu to the petition. When the chant is finished the dancers form themselves at the far end of the plaza and start a new episode.

This rather monotonous schedule of events is followed with little variation until the afternoon of the last day. Then all the *batana* and elders gather at one of the village temples for a special rite from which outsiders are strictly excluded. The women and children wait at the plaza in tense expectation. The sound of the horn is heard from the temple and the whole company of men come dancing towards the plaza singing a hymn. In their midst is a close cluster of about ten *wenamiji*, cloaks held above their heads, who are supposed to conceal Khambageu and conduct him to the sanctuary. The final dance then starts, and some of the women and children also take part in it. It is also customary for delegations of *batana* from other villages, properly dressed, to participate in the final

III*a*. *Batana* dancing at the Mbarimbari festival

III*b*. Girl in festival dress

dance—in fact they are welcome to join in any of the dancing sessions. At this point the plaza becomes crowded with a dense throng of dancers, and it is difficult to follow the formal action of the dance.

During the course of the festival all work of cultivation is suspended except for irrigation, which is carried on according to the regular schedule. The *vijori* remain at their goat camps tending their flocks, but an effort is made to rotate them in their duties so that everyone is able to be present in the village for part of the festival. The elders spend only part of their time at the plaza and for the rest of the time they lounge quietly in small groups at their homes talking, sipping beer, and receiving visitors from other villages. This is a time when old acquaintances are renewed and tribal matters are discussed in detail. The Masai of the region have a high regard for the Sonjo God and frequently come to the Mase festival where they are cordially received by the Sonjo, though at other times they are regarded with hostility. They bring offerings of goats and even fat-tailed sheep. Their petitions to Khambageu are said to be almost always for the birth of children. A number of Masai came to the festivals that we attended, but they tended to stay by themselves and appeared uneasy and forlorn. In addition to the public prayers and ritual, every individual is expected to pray silently to Khambageu at frequent intervals during the period of his presence in the village.

On the morning after the festival proper has finished, several goats are given to the young boys of the village for a feast which is held at one of the sacred springs. Not all the *vijori* are permitted to attend, but only those under the age of nine or ten of whom it is quite certain that they have not had sexual intercourse, which would bar them from entering the area of the spring. They are supervised by old men who are deemed past the age of sexual activity. This event brings to a close the Mase festival.

Shorter ritual

A third agricultural rite is performed when the sorghum crop in the *hura* fields ripens in February or March. As this date was outside the period of my field work, I did not witness the rite and will not attempt to describe it in detail. The rite, which is only a one-day affair, is called *Mbori-ya-hura* (literally 'goat of the irrigated land') and according to informants it is performed entirely by the *batana*. Each company of *batana*, both junior and senior grades, is given a goat by the *wenamiji*, so that in Kheri, with four wards, eight goats in all are slaughtered. These goats are demanded as tribute from the *wakiama* of the village unless the *wenamiji* happen to have a surplus of goats on hand from other sources. The *batana* consume the goats at a feast in the forest, then decorate themselves in much the same way as for the Mbarimbari festival and dance through the fields of ripe grain, performing certain ritual acts. In the evening there is dancing and singing at the village plaza.

A rite performed by the women of the village alone is said to be enacted several times a year. It is a fertility rite meant to produce an increase in the birth of children and livestock and in the yield of crops. It was performed once at Ebwe during my visit. On that occasion the women spent the morning at a temple that stands well above the other houses of the village. The men were not allowed to approach nearer than the village plaza. The women, naked to the waist and with their skins painted with red ochre, danced in the small courtyard before the temple, which appeared as a distant elevated stage from the viewpoint of the plaza. The priest officiating at the ritual did not show himself at the front of the stage. At about two o'clock in the afternoon the women put on their cloaks and came running down the steep path to the plaza singing and laughing. For the next hour they gave a public exhibition of intricate and lively folk dancing and singing in the plaza. First a large circle would be formed for a slow sedate dance. Then they would break up into groups of six or eight women who formed small circles and whirled wildly in ring-a-round-the-rosy dances until the circle flew to pieces or collapsed. After that the whole performance would be repeated with variations. Their songs were ribald in subject matter (so my informants explained) and there was much loud laughing and shouting. The men stayed at a discreet distance from the plaza and affected indifference, but nevertheless watched closely.

From time to time when special crises arise, such as droughts or epidemics, appropriate rites are performed, but these are

IV*a*. Dancers at the Mase festival

IV*b*. An elder demonstrating archery
technique

always adaptations of the basic ritual acts of sacrifices and
prayers to Khambageu. Finch (1957) has described sacrifices
carried out at shrines in and near the village of Soyetu for the
purpose of propitiating the sons of Khambageu who were
turned into stones by their father, but this cult does not seem to
be present at the villages of Kheri and Ebwe.

One of the *rites de passage* is an operation performed on
children with the object of producing permanent scars. As this
is associated with the mythology of the Khambageu cult it is
best described here. A small cut is made in the skin below the
left breast and over the left scapula and potash is then rubbed
into the wounds to delay healing and increase cicatrization.
This may be done any time during childhood, but if a child
shows any signs of mental abnormality the operation is performed immediately. The scar is called *ntemi* and is thought of
as the distinguishing mark of the Batemi or Sonjo. It is believed
that Khambageu will recognize his faithful followers by this
mark and save them at the end of the world. Thus, in so far as
it ensures salvation, the *ntemi* operation is viewed by the Sonjo
in a similar light to that in which baptism is regarded by
Christians.

Mention has already been made in chapter II and elsewhere
of sacred places and objects—springs, temples, shrines, rocks,
trees, and the like. There are strict taboos in connexion with
some of these places—e.g. the springs and guardhouses. These
places must be avoided by ordinary people at all times. Other
places are concerned in minor ritual, or in ritualistic acts. For
example, just inside the village gate at Soyetu there is a flat
rock called 'the meat stone'; any passer-by who is carrying meat
must place it on the stone for a moment before passing on. It is
believed that this is done in reverence for Khambageu, but the
special myth explaining the act is not known, at least by
ordinary people. I cannot say for certain that every sacred place
is the subject of special ritual, but the attitudes to these places
are themselves ritualistic. When an outsider visits a Sonjo
village these attitudes become very evident in the anxiety of
the people lest the visitor unwittingly profane some sacred place
and the precautions taken to prevent this. In fact where outsiders are concerned, the entire village is treated as sacred. The
villages were formerly completely closed to outsiders; as

recently as 1948 no strangers were permitted in a village during a festival;[1] and to this day no missionaries or teachers have been allowed to enter Rokhari.

The myths and rites that have been discussed up to this point are known by all adult men of the tribe. Sonjo informants state that there are still other rites which are performed secretly by the priests, but no detailed information about these secret rites was obtained.

PRIESTS

The Sonjo priests are known by two different titles. A consideration of the derivations of these terms reveals something of the character and function of the office of priest. The relevant paradigms are as follows:

1. *Mugwe*—God[2]
   Bugweni—temple; 'place of God'
   Bamugweni or *Vantu va bugweni*—priests; 'men of the temple'
2. *Khoro*—to sacrifice
   Khorowani—temple; 'place of sacrifice'
   Bakhorowa—priests; 'men who sacrifice'

The name Bamugweni is applied to the priests when they are considered as a clan; *bakhorowa* describes them as functioning in their priestly office. The priests constitute a clan in so far as they are an exogamous group recognizing patrilineal descent. They also have a territorial base at the village of Rokhari, where the section of the village containing the principal temples belongs to them. Unlike the other clans, however, many of the members live permanently in other villages where they reside in neighbourhoods belonging to different clans. At present there are said to be six fully qualified priests in residence at the temple ward of Rokhari, two assigned to each of the three temples. At least one more priest is in charge of the ordinary village temple

---

[1] A small pamphlet published by the Lutheran Church (Elikana *et al.* 1952) tells that when the first missionaries arrived at Soyetu a festival was in progress and they were not allowed to enter the village.

[2] A note on the word *Mugwe* is appended at the end of this chapter.

at Rokhari. The other villages appear to have from one to three priests each.[1] The priests marry wives from other clans in the usual way. Their sons inherit the office and become priests themselves. Daughters are married by men of other clans and thereafter have no special status.

The myth of origin of the Bamugweni clan was recounted in the section on solar myths. The goats owned by members of the clan are branded with a clan mark, as in the case of other clans. These goats are called 'Khambageu's goats', but in most respects they are managed in the usual way, and mingle at pasture with the goats of other owners. The goats which are brought to the village temple during the Mase festival as offerings to Khambageu—which add up to a substantial number—are believed to be taken directly up to heaven by Khambageu. The Sonjo are normally familiar with the individual features of all their own goats, but informants say that goats brought as offerings never appear in the herd of the village priests. While it is possible that the offertory goats from one village are transferred secretly to the Bamugweni of a different village, I have no verified explanation for the alleged disappearance of these goats. The priests own cultivated land and raise crops like other people. They are given preferred rights to irrigation water like the *wakiama*, but unlike the latter they are not required to pay tribute to the *wenamiji*.

The priests and their families are not supposed to wear anything but skin garments. Very recently some of the young sons of priests have been enrolled in the government primary school, and there they are required to wear either a cloth or a school uniform consisting of shorts and shirt. Thus there was a conflict in the two roles that these boys found themselves playing— students and priests' sons. A compromise was agreed upon whereby the boys changed costumes at a neighbour's house before starting to school in the morning, and on returning to the village in the afternoon they change back into skin garments before entering their own homes. The priests also wear a distinguishing decoration which is a metal bracelet on the left

---

[1] My informants from Kheri admitted that they were under strict orders not to divulge the names of priests or their number to outsiders, and evidently the whole tribe had been warned not to talk freely about this subject. Therefore my data are incomplete.

wrist.[1] This is only worn by qualified priests. Being a member of
the Bamugweni clan is a necessary prerequisite for a priest, but
by itself it does not automatically result in a boy becoming a
mukhorowa. In addition he must receive instruction and undergo
some form of initiation.

The sacerdotal duties of the priests are concerned mainly
with temple rites. They take little part in public ritual at the
village plaza. A priest is probably in charge of manipulating
the horn at the Mase festival and creating the 'voice of
Khambageu', but field investigations failed to establish this for
certain. Rites enacted at the temples are semi-private in
character. There the priest deals either with individuals or with
small exclusive groups. There is regular liaison between the
wenamiji and the priests, the latter being advisors on ritual
matters. According to informants the priests are repositories of
mythology and they are also experts on questions of theology.
However, ordinary villagers have little occasion to consult
priests on these matters. The Bamugweni are regarded as
prosperous but are said not to be the richest men of the tribe.
They are definitely subordinate to the *wenamiji* in terms of
political power.

OTHER CULTS OF THE SUPERNATURAL

Among African tribes whose environmental circumstances are
at all similar to those of the Sonjo certain complexes of supernatural beliefs are found so regularly that they can be regarded
as normal. The most important of these cults are concerned
with rainmaking, ancestral spirits, diviners and medicine men,
and witchcraft and sorcery. I shall comment briefly on these
four concepts as they appear among the Sonjo.

The subject of rainmaking was considered in chapter IV in a
discussion of the irrigation system. There it was pointed out that
no separate office of rainmaker, and no cult of rainmaking,
existed. It was suggested that rainfall was overshadowed by
irrigation water in economic and therefore ritual importance.

---

[1] Since guides and informants were reluctant to introduce an outsider to a
priest, it was only by these bracelets that I was able to recognize priests. On several
of these encounters I started conversations with them in an attempt to establish
cordial relations, but my overtures only met with rebuffs.

The psychological need for the assurance of supernatural aid in obtaining adequate rain, we noted, is served by the orthodox religious cult of the society.

The Sonjo believe in the existence of spirits or ghosts of the dead and call them *virioka*. These ancestral spirits should be remembered from time to time and offered a ritual libation of beer about once a year. This rite is normally performed by people for their own fathers. More remote ancestors are not believed to have power over their descendants and need not be remembered. If this minimum obligation to a dead father is neglected the ancestral spirit may bring illness to the son, or more likely to the son's children. This is not considered a very serious matter, though, and the sickness, if it is indeed caused by an ancestral spirit, should be cured by carrying out the libation. It is further believed that if a woman commits adultery, the spirit of her dead father or grandfather may cause her to have difficult labour at childbirth. Thus the ancestral spirits concern only the small lineage and not the whole clan. It is a household cult at most and of minor importance in the ritual life of the people.

A specialist who is supposed to have supernatural powers, and who is found in almost all Bantu societies, where he is called by the title *mwanga* or *muganga* or some cognate (cf. Johnston 1919), usually translated as 'diviner', is not found among the Sonjo. Herbalists and other medical specialists are regarded as skilled craftsmen rather than magicians. Except for the limited power of ancestral spirits to cause sickness, and the even more limited powers of witchcraft, the supernatural elements in the Sonjo medical system are all connected with the dominant cult. The only ritual customarily employed in the prevention and cure of ordinary disease are prayers and sacrifices to Khambageu.

The evidence is strong that beliefs in witchcraft have declined markedly in intensity during the last generation or two. Thus people are able to describe various methods of witchcraft and to explain how the art is transmitted from generation to generation, but they end up by stating that little or none of this is practised at present and that nobody fears witchcraft any more. Two kinds of practitioners in black magic were distinguished traditionally. A sorcerer (*mosakuti*) was one who

made charms or medicines for harming people. This is said to
be an extinct art at present. A witch (*mologi*) is a person who can
harm an individual by intentionally casting his evil eye upon
him. A few witches are supposed to be still practising their evil
art, but they are not very malevolent and can only harm small
children. It is believed that nearly always they would be
detected immediately because of their known hostility towards
the parent of the afflicted child and made to remove the harmful spell by spitting on the child. In former times, charges
against witches were discussed by the *wenamiji* in secret session.
Then at the end of a year all persons who had been judged
guilty of practising witchcraft during the year were summoned
before a meeting of the whole village and fined six goats apiece.
My informant from Soyetu, whom I estimated to be forty years
old, could remember the last of these witch-fining meetings to
be held in his village, which happened when he was a little boy.
The *batana* had been notified in advance and given the task of
rounding up the putative witches and bringing them before the
meeting. Six people were fined; the goats were turned over to
the *batana* to be used in feasts. Since then it is thought that
witchcraft has almost died out in the tribe, which is counted as
a blessing from Khambageu—a reward for attending faithfully
to the prescribed ritual.

An interesting aspect of Sonjo witchcraft is the belief that it
can only be inherited through the mother and that two witches
would never marry. If witchcraft were very prevalent, this
would mean that witches tended to form matrilineal lineages
with a suggestion of exogamy. This is the only trait that I found
to be associated with matrilineal descent.

STRUCTURAL INTERPRETATION

To what extent does religion affect the structure of Sonjo
society? One answer to a question of this kind was given by
Fustel de Coulanges in a pioneer study of the relationship
between religion and social structure in the ancient city-state.
He concluded that social forms associated with the religion
of the family were altered as that type of religion weakened,
and saw a simple causal relation between these concomitant
changes. 'Thus, by the single fact that the family no longer had

its domestic religion, its constitution and its laws were transformed' (Fustel de Coulanges 1956 : 396). On this question,
Durkheim took a position at the extreme opposite. Fustel de
Coulanges, he wrote, 'has mistaken the cause for the effect.
After setting up the religious idea . . . he has deduced from it
social arrangements, when, on the contrary, it is the latter that
explain the power and nature of the religious idea' (Durkheim
1947a : 179).

Both of these opposing interpretations are oversimplified and
overgeneralized as judged from the viewpoint of current anthropological thought. Religion and structure are not related to one
another as simple cause and effect. Rather it is a dialectical
relationship of mutual influences. At times they harmonize and
support one another; at times there is tension between them.
Applying Fustel's hypothesis to the Sonjo, we find that their
'domestic religion' (the ancestral cult) appears to have declined;
for it is now weak by comparison with other Bantu tribes, and
this suggests that it was formerly more vigorous. We also find
that kinship bonds are relatively weak and narrow in compass,
but this is certainly not a direct result of the decline in family
religion. As I shall indicate in the next chapter, there is good
evidence that the ecological adaptation of the society required
a social structure imparting a firm unity to the whole village;
this was achieved at the expense of constituent groups based
on kinship which were deprived of some of their social functions.
Village unity is enhanced by the Khambageu cult embracing the
whole society. The ancestral cult very likely declined concurrently
with the structural weakening of kinship and lineage groups.

Sonjo religion does appear to have some degree of autonomy,
however. We noted earlier that the Masai are permitted to visit
the villages during the Mase festival, and are even welcomed,
though at other times they are excluded and regarded with
hostility. In contrast to this, the missionaries, friendly in everyday life and generally welcomed at the villages, are excluded
from the religious festivals. The reason is that the Masai accept
to some extent the Sonjo myths and are willing to participate
in ritual, whereas the missionaries openly express their dis-
belief of Sonjo myths. On the days that religion reigns supreme,
even the bitter enemies of the Sonjo are invited to the villages
so long as they profess belief.

Religions may in varying degree affect the personal behaviour of individuals or the norms by which behaviour is judged. In a Sonjo village the people must live close together, confined by the encircling fortifications. The successful operation of the irrigating system demands constant close co-operation of all the villagers. In this situation, aggressive or disruptive behaviour is intolerable. Accordingly, the norms of interpersonal behaviour and attitudes demand politeness and tolerance: aggressive or vindictive behaviour is condemned. These norms are sanctioned by religious myth and belief. Although in everyday behaviour most people fall short of the norms, during the days of the Mase festival it is expected that behaviour will actually conform to the norms, not only overtly but in thought and feeling as well. Thus the rules governing the religious festival provide an explicit model of the kind of personal behaviour required for the particular social structure.

Sonjo religion is a conservative force which acts to maintain the *status quo* culturally and socially. In this respect, religion provides a safeguard against disastrous change; for the social and ecological adjustment of the society is so delicately balanced that any change might constitute a threat to the livelihood of the people. Resistance to technological change tends to be rationalized on religious grounds. An example is the deliberate rejection of hoes by the Sonjo. Some years ago government officials of the agriculture department issued two hundred hoes to the Sonjo in an attempt to induce them to replace their digging-sticks with more efficient implements. The women, however, flatly refused to use them in cultivation, and in time the hoes were converted into cymbals, which soon replaced an indigenous wooden clapper as a percussion instrument at certain dances. The clappers have completely disappeared, and I only know about them from the descriptions of informants. Digging-sticks are sanctioned in sacred myths, and besides they seem to be satisfactory implements for working the wet soil of irrigated plots. Similarly, the introduction of cloths and blankets to replace skin garments was at first resisted on religious grounds, and is still resented by conservative elders.

Another example of extreme conservatism is the reluctance of the Sonjo to raise cattle, although grazing conditions are favourable for this and the danger of Masai raids has virtually vanished. The government veterinary department has been trying to introduce cattle for a number of years, but for a long time the people refused them, ostensibly on the grounds that it was prohibited by their religion. The first man to acquire a few cattle, Ginoria Koroi, the leading Lutheran, was severely censured for this sacrilegious act. A few men have recently followed his lead, and cattle are now kept at two of the villages. In the old days of Masai raids, cattle keeping would no doubt have entailed a serious danger to the security of the village. The religious injunction then conformed to military realities. That it remained in force after it no longer served any useful social function is indicative of the relative autonomy and momentum of a religious idea.

The relation of religion to the irrigation system is exemplified in the reverent attitude towards springs, and the myths and ritual attached to them. Religion finds one of its roots in ecology, because of the unusual importance of a single resource, water, in the life of the society. Thus, religion asserts that irrigation water has a sacred source. Rain is much less obviously an essential resource, and we find no special cult of rainmaking. In fact, rain is ritually assimilated to irrigation water; in the phrase 'open the sluices of Belwa', which occurs in communal prayers, rain is represented as a heavenly irrigation system. The irrigation system also has a social dimension. It must be controlled and regulated to be effective. The *wenamiji*, who control the water, draw in part on religious ideas for their power. They are closely associated with a sacred resource and are believed to have inherited their legitimate powers from ancestors who were divinely appointed to their positions. Thus the village rulers are supported in their authority and privileges by a 'mythical charter', to use Malinowski's term. The *wenamiji* take a prominent part in village ritual and they are said to be in close liaison with the priests. They have every incentive to uphold the tribal religion, for the religion tends to uphold them in their political power. However, it was not my impression that the *wenamiji* consciously manipulate religious elements for their own advantage. Sonjo religion is not imposed on the people by the rulers. It is based on the assent of the whole population, and in any particular situation the *wenamiji* as well as ordinary people must submit to the traditional demands of religion.

I might mention one further effect of religion on Sonjo social structure. This is to serve as a cohesive agent in integrating the different villages into a larger tribal society. The basic beliefs, shared by all the villages, provide a set of mutual understandings as to moral behaviour and ultimate values, which strengthen sentiments of friendliness and neighbourliness within the tribe and set it off from other societies with different beliefs. The religious festivals are the principal occasions for large-scale social interaction between villages and thus function to preserve the uniformity of the culture and promote tribal unity. Fortes (1936) in a study of Tallensi festivals makes a similar interpretation. The Tallensi are divided into two autonomous divisions, antagonistic in some situations, but possessing a common culture and intermarrying. Annual ritual festivals are celebrated by each of these major divisions, the members of one division attending as visitors at the festival of the opposite division. Fortes concludes (p. 604) that 'Social cohesion . . . is no ultimate attribute of that society, but is achieved by specific social mechanisms such as those I have described'—i.e. the ritual festivals. Similarly with the Sonjo, the social integration of the villages, which are politically autonomous and economically self-sufficient, cannot be taken for granted. Religion provides some of the strongest forces of cohesion, welding them together into a single society.

NOTE ON THE WORD 'MUGWE'

A book about the Meru of Kenya was published recently by Father Bernardi (1959) with the title, *The Mugwe, a Failing Prophet*. Since *Mugwe* is the generic word for 'God' in the Sonjo language, the question arises as to the relationship, if any, between these identical words in the two societies. In both of these Bantu languages the plurals of Mugwe are formed in essentially the same way: Sonjo, *Bagwe*; Meru, *Agwe*. Among the Meru the word designates a hereditary official having the role of a kind of high priest and prophet. Each of the main subdivisions of the tribe has its own *Mugwe*, but the essence of the position, the *Ugwe*, is evidently conceived of as a unity. The elders say that 'the power of the Ugwe is one' (Bernardi 1959 : 8).

The Meru have two names for 'God'—the Bantu word *Murungu* and the word *Ngai* borrowed from Masai. Although Father Bernardi denies that the Mugwe is identified with God, he quotes statements of his informants indicating that this idea does exist. Thus, one of the elders said of the Mugwe: 'He is like God. . . . Men go as far as saying that he is their father or their God' (p. 126). Another informant stated: 'The *Mugwe* we also called our God. The reason why we called him our God was that whatever we wanted he did for us. He despised nobody' (p. 195).

This is reminiscent of the way the Sonjo speak of Khambageu and explain his apotheosis. Assuming that the word *Mugwe* in both languages derives from a common origin (and the present evidence is not sufficient to put this beyond question), then the similarities which I have indicated might suggest the existence of an ancient cult of a Man-God having the character of a benefactor or saviour. The original cult would have evolved subsequently in divergent directions leading to the present cults of the Sonjo and Meru. By this interpretation, the Man-God among the Sonjo would have become fully deified and assimilated to the general or abstract concept of God; while in the case of the Meru, the idea came to be embodied in the position of a hereditary religious official who retains elements of divinity from the original conception. I put forward this conjectural interpretation as an hypothesis which can be tested by the findings of future comparative research in East African religions.

Chapter VIII

POLITICAL CONSTITUTION

THE POLITICAL COMMUNITY

TERMS such as 'society' and 'tribe' which I have applied to the Sonjo have no very precise meaning in general usage, and certainly tell us nothing about the political condition of the group to which the term refers. A common language, culture, and religion may be shared by several social groups which are politically quite distinct and independent of one another. Even the practice of intermarriage resulting in kinship bonds between groups does not necessarily lead to their political unity. These observations, of course, beg the question of what is meant by 'political'; but before attempting to define that concept it will be useful for practical purposes to decide upon the social unit to which it is to be applied.

In a discussion of African tribal societies, Schapera (1956 : 8) defines a 'political community' as 'a group of people organized into a single unit managing its affairs independently of external control (except that exercised nowadays by European governments)'. The Sonjo village satisfies this simple definition at least as well as the groups to which Schapera applies it. The village, moreover, is a natural entity, clearly demarcated geographically as well as socially. To a high degree the villages are economically self-sufficient and politically autonomous. The irrigation system and land holdings of every village are entirely separate from those of the other villages. In warfare with the Masai each village had to fend for itself. The warriors of the tribe were organized effectively only on a village basis, and there is no tradition of joint military action among the villages, except that information about Masai movements gathered by the patrols of one village was shared by all the villages. Trade relations between villages are meagre, for there is little village specialization in handicrafts or natural resources. On the other hand, among all the villages there are strong sentiments of amity and a prevailing sense of tribal solidarity. The villages do not seriously compete among one another for advantages, and thus there is little occasion for inter-village discord to arise. However, the factors promoting tribal unity—a common religion, kinship bonds, and an age-grade system embracing the whole tribe—tend to be in non-political spheres of organization. Considering everything, political sovereignty resides in the village.

The right and ability to use force is often regarded as a distinctive feature of 'political' life. Thus Radcliffe-Brown (1940 : xiv) states as characteristic of political organization 'the organized exercise of coercive authority through the use, or the possible use, of physical force'. In the same place, he writes further that 'In dealing with political systems . . . we are dealing with law, on the one hand, and with war, on the other'. The forces of physical compulsion in a Sonjo village reside mainly with the warrior age-sets. In analysing the village political constitution, then, we should particularly note the control and application of this force both in war and in law. Now *law* as it exists in primitive societies is a notoriously difficult concept to define. In a review of this question, Hoebel (1954 : 18–28) cites a wide range of definitions: at one extreme law is identified with the complex written codes of western nations; at the other extreme it is simply equated with custom. As a working definition for the purposes of this chapter, I quote a statement by Max Weber (1958 : 180):

Law exists where there is a probability that an order will be upheld by a specific staff of men who will use physical or psychical compulsion with the intention of obtaining conformity with the order, or of inflicting sanctions for infringements of it.

These definitions should help us focus for the present on the distinctively political aspects of the institutions of Sonjo society.

Like anyone who writes about an African political system, I am indebted to M. Fortes and E. E. Evans-Pritchard (1940) for their pioneer investigation of the subject. If I do not make specific use of the ideas and concepts that they formulated in their essay it is because the Sonjo political system cannot be easily subsumed under either of the two types which they

K

define—stateless societies and societies with centralized governments. Viewed as a political system, Sonjo society is constituted
of six different but similar communities. There is no central
authority for the whole society. Considered separately, the communities lack the essential features of segmentary stateless
societies. Each community is unified under a central government with political power being assigned to a hereditary group
of elders. The government group is not organized in the hierar-
chical fashion characteristic of 'centralized states', and its
members are not interrelated by kinship or lineage bonds. The
typology of African political systems will eventually have to be
extended in order to embrace societies like the Sonjo.

CLANS AND WARDS

The Sonjo villages are divided into from three to six territorial
subdivisions or wards. These numbers are exclusive of the
special sections in two villages occupied by the smiths and
potters, which are not comparable to ordinary wards in the
characteristics with which we are now concerned. Each ward is
occupied by a single clan, though in some cases it includes a few
men outside the clan. Thus the village priests live in regular
wards but do not belong to the occupying clans. In the village
of Kheri,[1] besides priests, there was only one family of outsiders
living in a ward; these people are said to be one of the remnants
of a small clan whose members became diminished in numbers,
quarrelled, and divided themselves among different villages. If
a person is expelled from a village he is supposed to be able to
find a new home in some ward of a different village and attach
himself to the clan that lives there. This seems to have seldom
happened in recent times, and most of the wards investigated
were inhabited exclusively by the clan that was the proper
proprietor. Thus clan and ward are nearly identical in that
the male membership of both are the same in most instances,
but for analytical purposes I shall treat them as separate social
institutions.

   The clans are exogamous groups and bear the same names as
the wards with which they are associated. In some cases this

---

[1] As in some of the earlier chapters, the statements made in this chapter refer
to the village of Kheri unless otherwise specified.

name derives from a place name: thus the Watinaga and Bayasi clans of Kheri are named after the abandoned villages of Tinaga and Yasi. Other names are taken from legendary heroes who are supposed to have founded the clans: examples of this at Soyetu are the Vegumune and Basarunde clans which are named after the two characters mentioned in the myth of the origin of Soyetu—Mwegumune and Msarunde. There are no clan totems or taboos and no cult of ancestral spirits involving a whole clan. As the inhabitants of a ward, the men of a clan constitute a corporate group. Their ward represents more than just a place of common residence: it contains a series of valuable house sites, the ownership of which resides with the clan as a whole. All members brand their livestock with a clan mark. This does not mean that the goats are regarded as property of the clan; such may have been the case at some time in the past, but at present the custom is explained solely as having the practical function of eliminating confusion in the herding of goats. The goats of one clan are normally herded together in the same area of pasture, and when they become mixed with other herds the clan marks facilitate sorting out the animals. Except for house sites, the clan is not actually concerned in the ownership of property. Goats, beehives, cultivated plots are all owned by individuals and inherited within the small lineage group. Each clan has a recognized leader who has authority to settle disputes between members.

Since an individual becomes a member of his father's clan, there is a general understanding that the members of the same clan have descended from a common ancestor. But the native theory of descent is poorly developed and genealogical knowledge is shallow and inaccurate. The clans are not systematically divided into a hierarchy of segments in the manner that has been described, for example by Evans-Pritchard (1940) for the Nuer, by Fortes (1945) for the Tallensi, and by Winter (1956) for the Bwamba. The component parts of a clan are small lineage groups consisting as a rule of several brothers, their children, and their father, spanning three generations at most. This group normally occupies houses that are located in the same part of the ward and are adjacent to or at least near one another. The members are bound together by primary kinship ties, by common interest in property, which is normally inherited within the group, and by the sharing in the livestock paid in at the marriage of a daughter, and the mutual responsibility for providing bride-price for the marriage of sons. The genealogical relations existing between different lineage groups is not reckoned to be important, and there is no formal alignment of groups within the clan on a genealogical basis.

A survey of one of the three wards of Ebwe—a ward named Bwelebu—was carried out to determine the pattern of residence and leadership. The sixty-one houses of the ward are located along the paths, with no grouping in compounds, so that it is impossible to discern the lineage grouping by inspection of the houses alone. Figure 2 is a diagram of the ward showing the

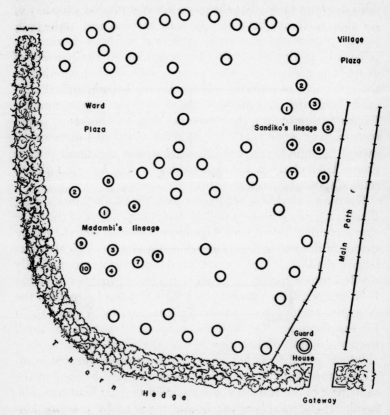

FIG. 2.   Diagram of Bwelebu ward in the village of Ebwe

distribution of houses. Ten adjacent houses near the ward plaza
belong to the lineage of the leader of the clan; this is the largest
lineage group in the ward. The genealogy of this lineage is
illustrated in Figure 3. The clan leader, Madambi, is an old
man living alone. His two sons are dead but their two widows
are living in separate houses near Madambi as his dependants;
each has an unmarried daughter. Madambi's two brothers are
dead but five of their sons are living, three of them with one
wife each and two of them with two wives. These sons could
not agree among themselves as to the name of their paternal
grandfather, and as Madambi did not make himself available
for questioning I was unable to determine the name of the
apical member of this lineage. The present coherence of this
lineage group is due primarily to the fact that Madambi has
no direct male descendants; his brothers' sons will ultimately

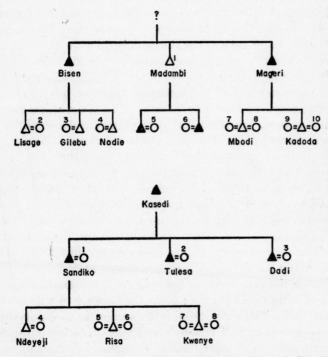

FIG. 3. Genealogies of the lineages of Madambi and Sandiko.
Numbers correspond to numbered houses in Figure 2

inherit his property, and already they are in possession of much
of this property. They also feel some personal obligation to
support Madambi as if they were sons, for he is a respected and
influential elder with no members of his immediate family
living in the village.

The second largest lineage group, occupying eight houses,
includes three elders—the sons of Sandiko—with their families
and some older women. Sandiko and his two brothers, who
formerly lived in that section of the ward, are dead, but the
three widows of these men remain, each living in her own
house. The genealogy of this family is indicated in Figure 3 and
the locations of their houses are shown in Figure 2. This group
retains its unity only by virtue of the common responsibility
of the three men towards the elderly widows of their father and
his brothers. It seems to be in the process of breaking up into
three new lineage groups. The elder whom I interviewed, Risa,
was uncertain about the name of his grandfather, Kasedi, until
he had consulted with his brother. Thus in these two lineages,
the active adult men of the lineage consider the name of their
grandfather to be of little importance and in some cases appear
to be ignorant of his name. My informants did not consider this
to be unusual. When the common economic interests among
lineage members disappear, and the name of the apical ancestor
is not known, the bonds between them dissolve rapidly, and
when another generation goes by the relationship between the
new lineages tends to be forgotten. Thus the clan lacks a
segmentary structure of linked lineages. Although members of
the same clan believe themselves to be descendants from a
remote common ancestor, the ritual features that are usually
found in societies with strong clan organization as expression of
the solidarity of the group—cults of ancestral spirits, totems,
and the like—are lacking in Sonjo clans. The bond uniting
clan-mates has relatively little mystical content.

When the same group of people are considered as members
of a ward instead of as clan-mates they appear as a more viable
social unit. The elder holding a position of authority in the
group, to whom I referred as 'clan leader' in earlier paragraphs,
is actually called 'ward leader' (montomolakolo wankai), which
is a more suitable title, considering that he lacks any ritual
function or supernatural sanction. His duties are essentially

those of a local magistrate and are secular in nature. He may
or may not be a member of the village council: Madambi is a
mwenamiji but some of the other ward leaders are not. The
people of a ward co-operate in everyday tasks: the women form
working parties to cultivate their fields, the herd-boys of a ward
tend to herd their goats together in the same area of the
pasture. Most of the secular dancing and singing of the Sonjo
occurs within the ward. Several times a week the young people
meet at the ward plaza in the evening for dancing. Each ward
possesses some special songs of its own.

Linton (1936 : 216–18) has described the universal tendency
of people to form themselves into 'neighbourhoods'—terri-
torially-based groups which are larger than the family but
usually smaller than the major political units of the society. The
size of a Sonjo village makes it difficult for an individual to
become intimately acquainted with all the other members.
Within a ward, however, this intimacy is quite possible.
Through frequent interaction and co-operation in work and
recreation, the members of a ward create an in-group sentiment
that satisfies the psychological needs for companionship and
emotional security that Linton describes. The ward members
live in contiguity and occupy a territory which is continuous
but not usually separated from other wards by natural features;
therefore the ward is based more on social needs than on
geographical contingency. Evans-Pritchard (1940) in analysing
the Nuer political system explains how the principle of 'opposition' distinguishes segments of a tribe and gives them unity. A
similar relation of opposition exists between the wards of a
Sonjo village, not in the serious spheres of political or economic
life but as competition between singing and dancing teams.
This competition together with the practice of exogamy, the
use of a common brand for goats, and the control of residential
sites, sets off the wards as completely distinct units.

The wards thus appear to be important and necessary subdivisions of the village. They are authentic structural parts
serving essential social functions; but since they are all very
much alike their relations to one another and to the village as a
whole tend to be mechanical, and thus the structure of the
wards cannot account for the organic unity which, as we shall
see, is characteristic of a Sonjo village. On the other hand, the

clan *per se* is incompletely structured into lineage segments and has few means of commanding the loyalty of members. Most of the functions which it serves—defining a sub-group of the society with its leader, providing a brand to distinguish the livestock of the group, organizing the people for co-operation in work and recreation—could be as well or better attributed to the wards without reference to unilineal descent groups.

Firth (1951 : 31) has stated as the 'essence' of structural relations that 'if such relations were not in operation, the society could not be said to exist in that form'. If we apply this criterion to the Sonjo clan it would appear that relations based on it do not possess the essence of structural relations. If the clans should cease to exist in the sense that the belief in unilineal descent should disappear, we can easily imagine that the society could continue to exist in much the same form as at present. The same people might continue to live in the ward grouped in homesteads of large families or small lineages, related to one another as members of a neighbourhood, and forming a corporate group, under the authority of a leader, with communal control of the rules of residence and the allotment of house sites. In only one important respect would there necessarily be change: the rule of exogamy could scarcely be maintained for long without the support of the incest prohibition based upon the belief in the common descent of all the members. And so with the introduction of intra-ward marriage, new forms of social alignment might be expected to arise. Therefore, if they are not entirely dispensable for the present form of society, at any rate the clans are structurally weak. I propose the hypothesis that they were formerly stronger in structure. As supporting evidence I shall only point out at this time that a rule of exogamy and the practice of marking livestock with a clan brand are incongruous customs in a descent group that has so little sense of lineage structure or group solidarity as the Sonjo clan, unless they are interpreted as survivals from a time when the clans were functionally stronger and served dynamic social functions. Later, as other parts of the village structure are analysed, I shall suggest further evidence for the hypothesis.

THE WENAMIJI

The authority possessed by this council of ruling elders resides with the group as a whole, not with the members as individuals. A chairman (*mwekorani*—a term also applied to the leader of an age-set) is elected from among the older members of the council to preside at meetings, but his opinion is supposed to have no greater weight than that of other members. The *wenamiji* hold meetings almost daily in the village plaza at which various aspects of the irrigation system are discussed and decisions made. The roster of individuals to be assigned irrigation periods is compiled at these meetings, and proposals for changes and adjustments in the schedule are made and decided upon. Daytime periods for irrigation are preferred to night periods for the obvious reason that people can then see better what they are doing. If a man draws several consecutive night periods he may specifically request and be granted a daytime period.

The *wenamiji* deal with all kinds of disputes and complaints about water at their meetings. The condition of the crops is discussed and the frequency with which they need irrigation decided upon. The status of the *wakiama* is reviewed and questions as to when to tax different individuals of that group are dealt with. Generally speaking, the transactions in which secondary water rights are dispensed to clients by individuals possessing primary rights are treated as private contracts to be settled between the parties concerned, but disputes arising out of these agreements may be mediated at the meetings. The council may listen to a case involving the abuse of water rights by a *mwenamiji* himself and may come to a decision that is against his interests. A *mwenamiji* may also be judged and fined by his fellow councillors for other offences which have nothing to do with irrigation. Although the regulation of the irrigation system is the most engrossing topic of these meetings, the council may at any time constitute itself a general court of law, and in formal meetings it also functions as the sole executive authority for the village.

The daily meetings are held at the restricted end of the plaza —the *khoseri*. Every member is expected to attend unless for good reason, especially if important matters are to be discussed. It is considered essential that all seventeen positions on the

council be filled by living members, and when a member dies
the council cannot hold meetings until his successor has been
initiated and installed in the empty place. The decisions of the
council are based on the democratic principle of equal votes
for all members. Normally a unanimous vote is desired on all
important questions; this may entail prolonged discussions and
attempts at persuasion when there is an initial disagreement
among members. As an individual, a *mwenamiji* has no special
authority over his fellow villagers. Administrative and disciplinary acts must emanate from the council as a whole gathered at a
formal meeting.

The other two categories of privileged men are allowed to
attend ordinary meetings, but they participate in the proceeding
in different degrees. The minor *wenamiji* may take part in
general discussions and make proposals, but they have no vote
on decisions. The *wakiama* are only allowed to listen, except
when they are permitted to testify in matters concerning their
own interests, such as the assignment of irrigation periods and
the assessment of tribute. Inside the *khoseri* there is a corral-like
enclosure which is only large enough to accommodate the
wenamiji, and which serves as a special committee room for
them. Here they retire when they wish to debate some question
in private. Affairs which only concern the *wenamiji* themselves
are also dealt with here—the collection and disposition of goats
from fines, tribute, and fees, the planning of sacrificial feasts
and special ritual, and the like.

Sonjo Law

The distinction made by Radcliffe-Brown (1933) between
'public delicts' and 'private delicts' can be conveniently applied
in classifying Sonjo legal procedures. Strictly private delicts are
rarely dealt with by the *wenamiji*. Bride-price is paid in full
before a marriage is consummated—a custom which tends to
preclude later disputes—and any disputes over inheritance are
settled by adjudication within the ward. Thus the two common
causes of litigation over property in African courts are virtually
absent from the Sonjo village court.

Purely public delicts fall in two categories. Anyone who is
charged with fighting or acting in any disorderly manner so that
he disturbs the peace of the village is subject to a fine of four

goats. The other category is a large one and includes all abuses of water rights. The most common of these offences is stealing water at night by illegally leading water from a nearby furrow and irrigating a plot. This delict, if detected, is punished with a fine of one goat, which is considered to be only a nominal penalty and well worth the risk if one's crops are badly in need of water. It is, of course, difficult to know how often water theft is successfully committed. My informants, one of whom was known as a frequent offender, assured me that it is very common indeed. It is curious that a crime which seems to strike at the heart of the system of authority based on the control of water should be frequently attempted and leniently punished when detected. An explanation is suggested by Max Gluckman in his study of conflict. 'Conflict in one set of relationships [he writes], over a wider range of society or through a longer period of time, leads to the re-establishment of social cohesion' (Gluckman 1955 : 2). Thus water theft can be thought of as an institutionalized form of conflict. The tacit acceptance by society that underprivileged cultivators may break the law to steal water with only a small risk renders the irrigation system more flexible and averts more serious conflicts if some of the men should lose their crops because of failure to obtain water legally. Other water offences are neglect of ditches for which an individual is responsible, improper use of sluices so that water goes to waste, failure to stop irrigating at the expiration of an assigned period, and any disobedience to an order issued by the *wenamiji*. The penalties for these misdemeanours are fines which vary according to the seriousness of the crime.

In former times all men judged to be guilty of witchcraft were fined six goats apiece at the end of the year, but this law has been inactive for a long time because of the fact, as it is believed, that serious witchcraft has died out during the last generation.

The most numerous offences are those treated as both public and private delicts. In these cases the guilty party is fined and the injured person is awarded compensation. The amount of the fine and compensation for the more common offences of this kind is fixed by a code which is briefly summarized below.

Homicide.—No distinction seems to be made between intentional and accidental killing; homicide of any kind is said to be

an extremely rare crime. It is regarded as primarily a ritual
offence, but is dealt with as if it were both a public and private
delict. The guilty person is fined thirty goats, six of which are
given to the survivors of the deceased, the other twenty-four
being kept by the *wenamiji*. All thirty goats, however, must be
slaughtered in successive sacrifices. When the sacrifices have
been completed, a committee of four *wenamiji* is appointed to
arrange a reconciliation ceremony between the two families
involved in the killing.

Certain kinds of personal injury are interpreted as intention
on the part of the aggressor to kill the injured person. The
specific injuries falling in this category are breaking a tooth,
injuring an eye ball, and breaking the loop of skin of an ear
lobe that has been pierced and stretched for the purpose of
inserting ornamental plugs. The penalty for inflicting these
injuries is the same as for homicide. The final reconciliation is
made between the two individuals—the aggressor and the
injured. By keeping firm control of these legal proceedings, the
wenamiji prevent the social disruption of a feud, which is a
potential result of homicide. This control is consolidated by
making the crime a grave ritual offence. If a person who was
found guilty of homicide or inflicting serious injury failed to pay
his fine, the sacrifices leading to reconciliation could not be
carried out. In that case special ritual sanctions would be
applied against him which, informants stated, would virtually
amount to excommunication.

Stealing.—Three kinds of theft are recognized as serious
offences and heavily fined. These are (1) stealing a goat and
then taking it to the forest to be killed and eaten in an illegal
feast; (2) stealing honey from a hive; and (3) stealing *hura* land
by moving a boundary stone into a neighbour's plot. The fine
in each case is twelve goats, which are divided evenly between
the owner of the stolen property and the *wenamiji*. Stealing grain
or sweet potatoes from a field carries a fine of two goats, one to
the owner and one to the village council.

Sex offences.—The case of an illegitimate pregnancy in which
the putative father is an uncircumcised boy was discussed in
chapter v: in a case of that kind there is no fine, but the
wenamiji supervise the necessary ritual purification and ensure
that the required marriage takes place. If an adult man is

judged to be responsible for a pregnancy in a married woman or a betrothed girl, he is fined twelve goats; the *wenamiji* keep six, as in the case of theft, and give six to the woman's husband or the girl's fiancé. Adultery is believed to be the only cause of difficult labour in childbirth. When this condition occurs, the woman is encouraged to confess any adulterous relations that she may have had before or during pregnancy. Her word is usually taken as conclusive evidence, and the man that she names is judged to be guilty. If more than one man is involved they must share the fine of twelve goats among them. If adultery can be proved against a man where no pregnancy results, the fine is only two goats, one to the husband and one to the council.

The village government takes no special part in a normal first marriage of a woman. Divorce and remarriage, however, are regulated by the *wenamiji* who charge the new husband a fee of seven goats to legalize the marriage.

Powers and privileges of wenamiji

The wide powers and special privileges of the *wenamiji* appear to be universally accepted as right and authentic and are not seriously questioned by anyone. The present members of the council were described by all informants as being the descendants in patrilineal line of a like number of men who lived in the days of Khambageu and were ordained in their positions by him. Thus their authority is bolstered by strong supernatural sanction. When informants discuss the functions of the *wenamiji* they stress their duties and special knowledge as much as their powers and privileges. These elders are believed to understand the irrigation system better than other people, and thus to be best qualified to control and regulate water. They were also regarded as the guardians of sacred tradition. Thus the welfare of the village and its very existence is thought to depend on them, not in the sense that there is a mystical bond between the *wenamiji* and the village, but because the irrigation system would collapse in chaos if it were not strictly regulated and if the proper relations between the village and supernatural powers were not maintained through proper ritual. The powers of the *wenamiji* receive further support from the existence of an accepted legal code. There is a reciprocal relation between the village rulers and the code: the law, although it allocates a preponderant share of political power and some special economic privileges to the *wenamiji*, is nevertheless conceived of as sanctioned by sacred tradition and as expressing the will of the whole village, not just the will of the council. The *wenamiji*, on the other hand, are the chief enforcers and administrators of the law. Thus the rulers uphold the law and the law uphold the rulers and confirms them in their authority.[1]

In enforcing their orders and decisions, the *wenamiji* rely strongly on the fact that the law commands the assent of the people, that their authority is regarded as valid, and that public opinion is usually behind them. Fines are not collected by forcible confiscation of property. If necessary, refractory individuals can be dealt with by refusing them irrigation water. The *wakiama* are particularly vulnerable in this respect, since they are dependent on the council as a whole for their special privileges, which are only temporary in any case and may be withdrawn if behaviour is unsatisfactory or tribute is not paid. Therefore the *wakiama* have a strong incentive to observe the law and give full support to the *wenamiji*. The minor *wenamiji*, on the other hand, are relatively free of control since their water rights are hereditary. The extreme sanction that can be applied by the rulers is expulsion from the village: when this is necessary, the *batana* are called upon to evict the offender and destroy his house.

As individuals, the *wenamiji* profit in two ways from their positions on the ruling council. In the first place they have special rights to the use of irrigation water and are free of the worry and insecurity of other classes of men (except for the minor *wenamiji*, who also have inalienable water rights). Individuals also receive small but welcome payments of honey from clients who apply to them for water. This is used for making honey beer, of which the *wenamiji* require relatively large amounts in order to celebrate festivals and offer hospitality as befits their social status. The second principal source of profit is the goats which are collected by the council as tribute, fines, and fees. These are believed to be used mainly in sacri-

---

[1] Max Weber (1958 : 180) writes: 'The structure of every legal order directly influences the distribution of power, economic or otherwise, within its respective community.'

fices, offerings, and ritual feasts which are supposed to benefit the whole community, and in fact most of these goats are consumed in that way. Other people in the village are sometimes allowed to partake of the ritual feasts, but the *wenamiji* are assured of the largest share. The raw meat of sacrificial animals is sometimes divided among the officiating elders who take it home and distribute it to their families and neighbours. My wife and I were sometimes sent a portion of a sacrifice from Kheri with the compliments of the council. Tribute from the *wakiama* is collected only when goats are needed for some special ritual purpose. If a number of goats accumulate from such sources as the payment of fines and remarriage fees, they may be divided among the individual *wenamiji* who add these animals to their personal herds. In theory these remain the joint property of the council and may be demanded if needed for some ritual use; otherwise they are forgotten in time and remain the property of the individual.

From the data that are available it is impossible to estimate accurately the total number of goats that the council normally collects in a given period of time. A certain number of these goats are transferred to the village priests and to the priests in charge of the central temple at Rokhari, but these transactions are shrouded in secrecy so that detailed information is lacking.

Succession to office

When a *mwenamiji* dies his successor is invested with the office as early as possible, usually within a week or two of the death, for in the meanwhile the council members are not supposed to meet and the village is thus without a government. A brother or eldest son is the normal heir. Before a new member can be initiated the funeral rites for the deceased must be completed. Traditionally the rites for an important man, such as a village councillor, lasted eight days, but at present has been shortened to about three days. Then, after an interval of a day or two, the candidate must produce an initiation fee consisting of one goat, one fat-tailed sheep, and four jars of honey—the total value of this is equivalent to seven ordinary goats. As soon as the honey has been brewed into beer the candidate is initiated in a ritual enacted at the spring associated with the clan of the dead man and his successor. The animals are slaughtered; long prayers are chanted in which the dead man is eulogized, the candidate is commended to Khambageu for guidance, and blessings are requested for the village; then the meat is roasted and the elders settle down rather solemnly to drink beer and feast. Unlike some of the other ritual, this affair is not strictly private: I was invited to attend one of the initiation rites as a guest, and was given a portion of meat and a small gourd of beer when I left. Within the next day or two the *wenamiji* meet formally at the *khoseri* and receive the candidate as a new member.

At the time that a candidate presents his initiation fee, one of his brothers (normally the next in seniority) has the option of contributing one goat towards the fee and thus establishing his claim to be next in line of succession to the membership. If no brother does this the membership will automatically descend to the eldest son. The membership is the possession of the lineage group in which only a small span of kinship is recognized, though the limits are not rigidly fixed. It is possible under unusual circumstances to sell the rights to the office of *mwenamiji*, and a case of this kind happened recently. At present there are two full brothers among the Kheri *wenamiji* —Ngadi and Ngeya, the sons of Webu. This family acquired its second membership in the following way. The only surviving heir of a *mwenamiji* was a brother named Kadeba who was very poor in goats. He decided not to accept the membership but to move with his family to Kenya to work for a lumber company in the Mau Forest. (Agents of this company occasionally recruit labour from among the Sonjo.) He put his membership up for sale and it was purchased by old Webu for his eldest son Ngadi. As tradition demanded, he paid Kadeba a sum of fifteen goats and also paid fifteen goats to the *wenamiji*. Later he died and his second son Ngeya inherited his own membership.

The death of a minor *mwenamiji* is followed by proceedings and ritual similar to those for a *mwenamiji* proper, but it is less disrupting to communal life as the village government is not interrupted. The successor in this case pays exactly the same initiation fee. The ritual at the clan spring is attended by the *wenamiji* proper as well as the minor *wenamiji* and both groups share in the meat and beer.

Clan representation in village government

The village of Kheri is divided into four wards with four corresponding clans named Wakifuna, Basakhabu, Watinaga, and Bantubeeti. The Bantubeeti clan has five members on the village council, the other three clans four members each. Thus the seventeen *wenamiji* are divided as equitably as possible among the clans. In this village there is no ranking of clans on the basis of seniority or other criteria of superior status or strength. Judging from these data alone, one would be inclined to think that representation on the village council was of considerable importance to the clans, and that the even distribution of political power among the clans was the result either of deliberate agreement or of mutual limitations by competing groups who were jealous of each other's power and privileges. At Kheri these factors may possibly operate to some extent, perhaps more in the past than at present. But the Sonjo deny that the *wenamiji* are primarily representatives of their clans or that a clan as a whole derives any special benefit from having their members on the council. The equality of clans and equal distribution of council memberships found at Kheri is not a universal feature of Sonjo society. At Soyetu the situation is quite different. At that village there are six clans, with three of them being ranked as major clans and the other three as minor clans, the distinction being made mainly on the criterion of numerical strength. Two of the major clans and two of the minor clans possess *wenamiji*, and one clan from each category lacks any *wenamiji*. There are eighteen members of the council altogether. The actual distribution of memberships among the clans is listed below.

Major Clans	*Wenamiji*
Egemune	9
Goleda	0
Kirigurune	5
Minor Clans	
Sarunde	2
Mererane	0
Goenga	2
Total	18

L

The situation at Soyetu provides evidence supporting the native interpretation that the *wenamiji* are constituted primarily as a unified village institution rather than as a council of clan leaders. It illustrates that a clan, such as the Goleda, can prosper and be regarded as a major clan without having any direct representation on the village council. In common opinion the *wenamiji* are thought to act solely for the benefit of the whole village. The rewards which accrue to the *wenamiji* are enjoyed for the most part by the members jointly as an exclusive group and are not transferred to the clans which they represent. The personal privileges of the office are shared by the immediate families of members—their wives and children—and to some extent by the small lineage group, but they do not tend to diffuse further along lineage lines.

THE BATANA

We noted in chapter VI that the age-grade system extends through the whole tribe, but that the only effective organization of the age-sets is within the villages. Here we shall consider the role played by the warrior classes in the political structure of the village. As a distinctive group within the village the *batana* possess two characteristics which are relevant to their political role: (1) they are primarily warriors and constitute the only organized military force in the village; and (2) as individuals they are relatively separated from other social and economic institutions of the village. The *batana* live away from their families, and for the period of their warriorship many of the normal obligations of kinship are placed in abeyance. Their involvement in the economic system is minimal and they are not normally concerned with questions of irrigation or goat ownership. Thus their viewpoint and motives are somewhat different from those of other adult men of the village.

The structural functions of the warrior classes in village government are of two kinds. In the first place they represent a police force that is obedient to the ruling group and ready to enforce its orders. The ultimate sanction of the *wenamiji* is the expulsion of a recalcitrant or rebellious individual, and the physical force behind this sanction is supplied by the *batana*.

The physical force possessed by the *batana*, and also their obedience to the village rulers, is symbolized in the role which they play at important village festivals. There the formal dancing, which is the most impressive public ritual of the festival, is performed almost exclusively by the warriors arrayed in special costumes suggestive of their military character. The warriors feel that they are acting voluntarily in their traditional and proper role and participating fully in an important aspect of village life, and yet the ceremonies are supervised and regulated by the *wenamiji*.

Secondly, the *batana* constitute a corporate group possessing real power which potentially might be used in enforcing its own will independently of other groups. When the warriors desire some action on the part of the village government or have some grievance that they want to bring to the attention of the village, they make their wishes known by a certain programme of group behaviour. First they retire to a camp in the forest and discuss the question until a unanimous agreement is reached either to act a resolution or to dismiss the matter. If the decision is to act, then for several nights they perform certain dances in the village, which informs the people of their intention of demanding some action from the village council. The leaders of the different warrior companies present the resolution to the *wenamiji* at one of the regular morning meetings. The *wenamiji* are expected to give careful consideration to the resolution and to act upon it unless there are strong reasons against it. This behaviour by the *batana* implies an intimidation of the village rulers by a show of force. Shortly after my arrival in the field, the warriors of Soyetu took action of this kind. There had recently been a bitter controversy in the tribe over granting the Catholic Church permission to establish a mission station near Soyetu. The *batana* of that village identified themselves with the pro-Catholic party and decided to demand the expulsion of one or two of the leading Lutherans from the village. There was the traditional dancing for two nights, then the resolution was formally presented. Plans had already been made to drive these people from the village and burn their houses. The *wenamiji*, however, persuaded the leaders of the *batana* that the plan was unreasonable, and the demand was finally withdrawn.

Warfare

The manifest function of the age-sets—and one that in the recent past was essential for the very existence of Sonjo society —was to protect the villages against attacks by the Masai. The military organization of the *batana* and their duties and activities as warriors have already been discussed. It will be recalled that the duties of patrolling the region and guarding the village gates occupied much of their time, and that they took almost no part in the economic activities of the village. In a sense, their role was that of a professional army which is devoted exclusively to military affairs and supported economically by the civilian population. The supreme command of this army lay with the *wenamiji*, who were also the makers of military policy, but all subordinate positions of command were occupied by the *batana* themselves as village and company leaders of the two warrior classes. In time of actual attack the 'regular army' was reinforced by the other adult men of the village, all of whom possessed weapons and remained practised in their use. The whole force was then posted to definite positions in the village according to a previously planned scheme of defence. Evidently this efficiently organized system of defence was nearly always successful in repulsing the enemy, in spite of the cunning and courage of the Masai *moran*.

In summary, one of the necessary conditions of existence for a Sonjo village was an effective system of defence against Masai raids, and the warrior age-class fulfilled this condition. As a consequence of their mode of life and military functions, the *batana* are relatively free of the vested economic interests which involve all the older men of the village. They are detached from the status system which centres on irrigation rights. The *batana* as a group are primarily related to the village as a whole rather than to special factions or classes. The considerable power possessed by the *batana* is aligned with the authentic government of the village, but the group is capable of manifesting some degree of autonomy. The organization of the warrior classes and their relation with other groups have the effect of strengthening the unity of the village and also the unity of the whole tribe.

SOCIAL CLASSES

The older adult men of a village can be divided into several groups according to the kind of rights to irrigation water that each possesses. These rights were discussed in chapter IV in an agricultural context. The different categories or classes of water-users described there were the *wenamiji*, the minor *wenamiji*, the *wakiama*, and the clients. To this number we can now add the priests, who form a special class of men with respect to water rights. In addition, there are two other classes —the Waturi or smiths and the military age-sets—who are without water rights as they do not take part in cultivation; these will be disregarded for the time being. The diagram in Figure 4 is a representation of the system of water rights, with the arrows indicating from whence the rights originated and upon whom they are conferred. The multiple arrows signify that individuals rather than whole groups are involved in the transfer of rights: this is the case in every transaction except where the *wenamiji* act as a unit in assigning rights to individuals of the *wakiama* group. Individuals of the *wenamiji* and minor

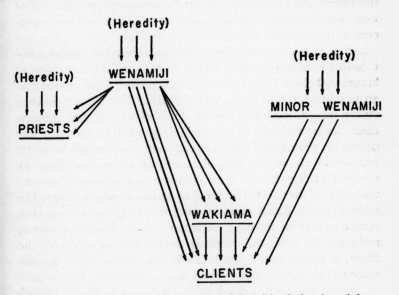

FIG. 4. Diagram of social classes as defined by irrigation rights

wenamiji groups acquire their water rights by inheritance from their patrilineal predecessors. A double origin is indicated for the water rights of priests: they acquire their positions as priests by lineal succession, and as such they are entitled to special consideration from the *wenamiji* who control and regulate the water.

The structural relations between these groups, as indicated by the arrows of the diagram, are polarized in terms of super-ordination and subordination, with the arrows pointing to the subordinate member of the relationship in every case. Thus the *wenamiji* are superordinate to all other groups, the clients are subordinate to all others, and the *wakiama* are subordinate to the *wenamiji* but superordinate to the clients. The relations of the minor *wenamiji* are less sharply defined in these terms. Their water rights, though hereditary, are subject to regulation by the *wenamiji*. There are no direct relations between them and the *wakiama* based on water rights. The priests are so few in number and so specialized in social function that they are not an important factor in the system of irrigation rights.

Another way of stratifying the population could be based on the ownership of livestock, goats being the principal form of wealth among the Sonjo. Unfortunately, reliable data concerning goat ownership are lacking, for the Sonjo, like many other stock-herding peoples in Africa, are reluctant as individuals to tell how many animals they own. In the opinion of informants there is no significant difference in the numbers of goats owned by *wakiama* and *wenamiji*. The former have a strong incentive to acquire this form of wealth and increase their flocks, for by owning enough goats they can pay the necessary tribute and thus acquire rights to the use of water which are almost as valuable as those of the *wenamiji*. To obtain these rights they must compete among themselves and with clients, for the line dividing these two classes is permeable, allowing some social mobility both upwards and downwards. A *mokiama* whose livestock decreases may no longer be able to maintain his position, which is then taken by a prosperous client. It is said that a family is often required to give up possession of the position of *mokiama* when the father dies; for after his wealth has been divided among the sons no one of them is able to afford the tribute necessary to maintain the position.

There are other advantages attached to goat ownership besides the ability to purchase water rights. Thus only wealthy men can produce the large number of goats required for multiple wives. Goats can also be exchanged for other commodities, for grain in time of food shortage, and for honey which is made into beer and permits the owner to entertain other elders and thus build up his prestige in the village. To some extent all the men of the village compete against one another for these goods, but the *wenamiji* have less need for personal wealth than other classes. Their desires for feasting and beer-drinking are largely satisfied through ceremonial feasts of the whole council, paid for out of communal wealth; and superior prestige is already attached to the office of *mwenamiji* so that the distribution of largess is not necessary on the part of individuals. Sonjo bride-price is comparatively high and it varies so widely that the highest bride-price is several times as great as the lowest. This variation does not seem to be determined by the personal desirability of a bride, because most betrothals take place when the girl is still a child. It is determined rather by the social and economic status of the girl's family. This sliding scale of bride-price should tend to promote marriages within rather than between classes, but the data now available are not sufficient to permit an empirical test of the extent of this tendency.

In summary, individual wealth, measured by goat ownership, is overshadowed by the system of irrigation rights as an economic basis for social stratification. Water as a resource is susceptible of monopolistic control in a way that goat ownership is not. The classes defined by irrigation rights tend to coincide with those based on personal wealth, but the correlation is not perfect. Political power is derived predominantly from the irrigation system and only in small measure from the system of goat ownership. The ruling class controlling irrigation water is a corporate group with closed membership. The minor *wenamiji*, who have guaranteed water rights but no special political power, are also a closed group, and so are the priests. Other closed groups are the Waturi and the *batana*, but these people do not practise cultivation and thus stand outside of the system of water rights. The remaining classes, whether defined by different irrigation rights or personal wealth, are open classes between which mobility is possible for individuals; they are not corporate groups and are incapable of unified action.

SUMMARY OF POLITICAL CONSTITUTION

The village is divided segmentally into clans and wards which are equivalent units related to one another in an essentially mechanical way, so that they do not much enter into the strictly political functioning of the village. Because of their weak internal structure, the clans have few functions that are not also possessed by the wards considered as territorial units without regard for the belief that the members constitute a unilineal descent group. Political power and authority is preponderantly in the hands of the *wenamiji*. This power is derived mainly from the control of irrigation water in a way that was discussed in chapter IV and earlier in this chapter. The power of the *wenamiji* is reinforced by mythological charter, by close association with religious ritual, and by the legal framework of the society. The *wenamiji* administer the law and are upheld by the law. The physical force of the village is provided by the *batana*, who constitute an army and police force under the command of the rulers. The majority of the men of a village belong to two classes—*wakiama* and clients—which are formally defined in terms of irrigation rights. Only the wealthier men (measured by goat ownership) can afford to pay tribute to the *wenamiji* and thus become *wakiama* with superior rights to water. The ownership of goats is desired because of various advantages, but the main advantage is the ability to purchase water rights. Thus the irrigation system serves as a basic determinant of class structure as well as the source of political power.

Chapter IX

CONCLUSIONS

ECOLOGY AND SOCIAL STRUCTURE

HAVING completed my presentation of field data, I shall now attempt to formulate some conclusions by reviewing my findings in the light of the theoretical concepts discussed in the Introduction. There I stated my intention of following as a general guide Steward's 'ecological method' which involves a three-stage programme of investigation. Steward's first procedure requires the analysis of the 'interrelations of exploitative or productive technology and environment'. The arid environment of the Sonjo, as we noted, is suitable for two forms of exploitation—stock raising and cultivation by irrigation. Both forms are practised by the Sonjo and constitute the basis of their subsistence economy. In utilizing as goat pastures the natural grasses and shrubs that the environment offers the Sonjo obtain an important portion of their food supply and the goat skins which are used for garments and technical equipment. It is noteworthy that no basketry of any kind is made by the Sonjo, although this art is highly developed among the related Ikoma. The environment is lacking in swamp grass and reeds which are commonly used in East Africa for making larger baskets. The Sonjo satisfy their need for basket-type receptacles by making goat-skin containers of various sizes and shapes. Although Sonjo stock raising can be interpreted as a response to the challenge of the physical environment, this response was modified and limited by the human environment; for the proximity of the predatory Masai prevented the Sonjo from keeping cattle.

For agriculture, the environment offers the two resources of soil and water. The Sonjo manipulated these two elements to create a system of irrigation which has been efficient and flexible enough to sustain the population. In the dry season they cultivate the rich but limited land of the valley bottoms, irrigating it with the relatively stable water supply of springs. In the rainy season they cultivate other crops by making use of the scanty rain—which in itself would not be adequate—and supplement it with as much irrigation water as can be brought to higher land. These crops are subject to greater fluctuation, but the valley-bottom crops provide security in dry years and there is no tradition of outright famine due to crop failure in recent years. The technical equipment of agriculture is extremely simple, but appears to be adequate for exploiting the arable land. The exploitative technology of the Sonjo requires little comment, though its simplicity is perhaps deceptive. Rather than elaborate equipment, the most important elements are knowledge and sound judgement as to water control, seeds, crops, seasons, and the various operations of cultivation. In addition to pasture lands and arable land, the Sonjo also exploit the resources of fields and forest for building materials and some of their less fundamental needs such as honey and herbs.

The next step in Steward's programme is the analysis of the 'behaviour patterns involved in the exploitation of a particular area by means of a particular technology'. By following this procedure, the population can be divided into four groups according to their participation or lack of participation in the major exploitative tasks. Starting with goat raising, we find that the work is done almost entirely by uninitiated boys—the *vijori*. Although no highly specialized skills are required in herding goats, still a body of fundamental knowledge must be mastered to ensure the health, increase, and safety of the herds. Much of this knowledge and lore is possessed by the boys themselves and is passed on to young recruits with little outside help or interference. Inasmuch as they, and they alone, are almost exclusively concerned with the technique of goat herding, the *vijori* constitute a distinct segment of the population with norms of behaviour which differ in some ways from other groups. After the *vijori* are initiated as *batana* and enter the warrior class they have little to do with goat herding. The *batana* are distinguished as a group, according to our present scheme of classification, by their lack of participation in the major exploitative activities. They are, however, essential in the military system —also necessary for the existence of the society—and play an important part in the political structure. Steward's ecological method alone would not disclose the role of the *batana*.

The third group with special behaviour patterns related to a mode of exploitation are the women of the tribe, who perform all the routine tasks of cultivation. Considered in this light they are comparable, *mutatis mutandis*, to the *vijori*, only they possess a wider age span and their mode of passing on special knowledge and skill tends to be channelled more in family lines: mothers normally teach their daughters the arts of cultivation. The adult men of the society, after they have left the warrior grade, devote themselves to the manipulation of irrigation water as their special exploitative activity, and they have only supervisory relations with the other groups. The distinctive behaviour patterns of these groups as they are engaged in their various tasks were discussed in the text.

Steward's last procedure requires much more complex analysis than the other two. It is 'to ascertain the extent to which the behaviour patterns entailed in exploiting the environment affect other aspects of culture'. In carrying out this procedure we are dealing in the main with the 'latent functions' (in Merton's sense) of exploitative behaviour—its effects on other aspects of culture which are not consciously intended by the people concerned. These effects of the ecological situation have been indicated in a number of places in the study. Here we shall consider in review only some of the more direct consequences of the exploitative behaviour described in summary fashion in the preceding paragraphs. For example, the *vijori* in their specialized task of goat herding incidentally undergo a course of training in fieldcraft, self-sufficiency, and physical courage which prepares them for the role of warrior which follows next in their lives. Later, when they become elders, they will make use of their knowledge of goats, gained when they were young, in carrying out various exchanges and transactions involving goats; for besides providing the elementary resources of food and skins, goats have other economic and social functions. Thus they serve as a standard of value in the operation of the simple exchange system for the distribution of goods. Certain fundamental social relationships are created or strengthened by the transfer of goats, as in the bride-price paid at marriage and the property which passes through lineage lines in inheritance.

Class status depends partly upon ownership of goats, though this status is determined primarily by irrigation rights. Finally, all important religious offerings and sacrifices involve the transfer of goats. In serving these secondary social and religious functions, goats become to some extent symbols: that is, they are visible manifestations of relationships or values which exist independently in non-economic spheres of the society. Goats are not just arbitrary symbols, however, and their economic or utilitarian value, grounded in the ecological situation, carries weight whenever there is exchange or transfer of goats, whatever the purpose of the transaction.

Turning to the exploitative behaviour of women, it is not difficult to trace the main effects of this behaviour in non-exploitative aspects of society. After her functions as sexual partner and mother of children, a woman is valued for the skill and labour which she brings to bear on food production. In some cases this value may be regarded as paramount, because the need for food is often more immediate and relentless than for sexual satisfaction. Since men themselves do not cultivate, every man is dependent on one or more women for his supply of vegetable food. Ability to perform her food-production role satisfactorily adds to a woman's value as a wife while failure to do so may be a cause of divorce. Since women as the cultivators are more intimately aware of the need for fertility in crops, they are entrusted with the specific fertility ritual, and by participating in tribal religion thus achieve closer integration into the total society. Grain and other vegetable foods, produced by women, are not normally exchanged to any great extent, and, unlike goats, they seldom function as symbols for other relationships and values. They are consumed and valued mainly within the family or lineage group and serve to strengthen the solidarity of that group, which is the fundamental building block of the social structure.

Irrigation, the work of men, was selected for special study and my analysis of a Sonjo village was largely based upon this aspect of ecological exploitation. A final summary of the subject will be drawn up when we again review the hypotheses of Wittfogel which were discussed in the Introduction. Thus I have attempted to account for much of Sonjo social structure through following the ecological methodology outlined by

Steward. A thorough application of the method should lead to the study of most aspects of a society, but it could not entirely account for elements which derive from historical contingencies, or which are the consequence of the human environment —that is, of other groups interacting with the exploiting group being studied. In the case of the Sonjo, the most significant of these factors is the Masai, and we must now consider briefly the effects of these neighbours on the Sonjo.

In some ways the needs for irrigation and for defence against the Masai have had similar effects on social structure. Thus the Sonjo settlement pattern—living in compact villages—was necessary in order to protect the people and livestock from Masai raiders, but it is also a very suitable arrangement for the type of agriculture which the environment demands. The cultivated fields are all concentrated in circumscribed continuous areas to which water can be applied, and it is convenient for the people who cultivate one of these areas to live together in a village located near their cultivations but not occupying arable land. Masai pressure, however, necessitated defensive palisades surrounding the villages, and this in turn induced the inhabitants to live as closely together as possible, which probably resulted in a higher population density of the dwelling areas than would otherwise have been necessary. To produce flat terraces for house sites on the rocky hillside required a great deal of labour which would probably not have been expended had the people been free to disperse and search for natural terraces as house sites. Because of this labour, the house sites represented economic values under the control of the clans. Thus the clans were indirectly strengthened by having this function of strictly regulating residence thrust upon them by the needs for efficient defence arrangements.

A response to the Masai that has more social significance was the development of a military age-grade system. If we imagine the Sonjo as having lived in their present environment, but in a milieu of peace instead of in constant danger of attack, there would be few functions for the warrior class to serve, and the age-grade system would certainly not exist in its present form. This system has been influenced by the Masai in two ways: first, it was a response to the need for a military organization of some kind which would be effective enough to repel Masai raids; secondly, some of the features of the system seem to have been borrowed directly from the Masai. Most of the borrowed traits, however, are comparatively superficial, and the differences between the two systems are considerable. From what we know of the Masai age-grade organization[1] it seems to be the principal factor operating within the tribe, or even within major territorial subdivisions, to integrate the society; whereas the Sonjo age-sets are definitely secondary to the organization of the village elders as factors in social integration. The predominantly military function of the age-grade system is evident in the fact that an age-set loses most of its distinctiveness and coherence after the members pass from the grade of senior warrior to that of elder; thereafter they do not constitute a corporate group. In its internal organization an age-set parallels the general territorial organization of the tribe and does not add any new principle. A single set extends through the whole tribe but, like Sonjo society as a whole, it lacks a central authority or unified organization. Effective organization of the age-sets exists only at village level, and the village group, like the villages themselves, is formally subdivided into ward units.

In its traditional form, the Sonjo warrior class tied up a large amount of potential labour which might otherwise have been applied to exploitative activities. Setting the average age at which a young man leaves the warrior class at about twenty-seven, this means that seven or eight years of his adult life are devoted to non-economic activities. In reviewing Sonjo ecology, it is difficult to see where this additional labour could have been applied had it been released from military service. As it is, the elders of the tribe are by no means effectively employed at economically rewarding activities. Thus the irrigation methods of the Sonjo appear to provide a relatively efficient mode of food production in terms of labour output. At present with the breakdown of the age-grade system, some of this potentially productive labour is being applied as migrant labour in non-traditional economic activities, and it could be predicted with considerable confidence that if the age-grade system disintegrates completely the labour of young adult men

---

[1] This statement is based mainly on personal communications from Mr. Alan Jacobs who has completed a field study of this aspect of Masai organization.

that is released will be employed either outside the tribal area or in some new mode of production introduced into the area from outside.

HYDRAULIC THEORY APPLIED TO THE SONJO

Let us now consider again some of the general hypotheses discussed in the Introduction concerning the characteristics of irrigation societies in general. The first hypothesis, stated by Steward, suggested a relation between environment and technology in simple irrigation-based societies. The significant part of his statement reads: 'The environments . . . did not impose great difficulties. . . . Instead, they facilitated culture growth because they were easily tilled by digging-stick and irrigation farming' (Steward 1949 : 7). The Sonjo data tend to support this statement. The technical equipment used by the Sonjo in cultivation is of the most primitive kind. The only implement used in preparing the fields, planting seeds, and cultivating the growing crops is the digging-stick. This has proved so adequate to the needs of Sonjo agriculture that the people have been able deliberately to reject more advanced implements, such as the iron hoe, although they are now obtainable and have been urged upon the people by government officials. The only other tool used in the fields is a small iron knife for cutting ripe ears of sorghum or millet. It would make little difference in the work of harvesting if these knives were replaced by stone knives or sickles with microlithic blades, in which case the agricultural operations would be performed entirely with neolithic equipment. Digging-sticks are also the traditional implements used in constructing and maintaining the irrigation furrows, and only in the last few years have some of the men started using hoes.

Therefore, since the Sonjo are more archaic in their cultivating tools than neighbouring tribes which do not practise irrigation, it is safe to conclude that their present social forms are not the result of a revolution in technical equipment. Wittfogel (1956 : 155) offers a similar interpretation of hydraulic societies in general: he writes that they came into being 'not through a technological but through an organizational revolution'. We turn now to those hypotheses of Wittfogel which were discussed

in the Introduction. They are concisely restated immediately
following and again numbered in the same sequence.

1. *The specific qualities of water as a resource affect the organization
of a hydraulic society.*—This is such a broad generalization that
it has only limited analytical value. Because of their dependence
upon irrigation the Sonjo can only cultivate the land that lies
below the level of the sources of water supply. This limits the
amount of land that can be cultivated and the population that
it supports. The settlement pattern of the Sonjo is adapted to
the hydraulic aspect of the ecology, but was also modified by
their need for defence against the Masai. The manipulation of
water as a resource requires the co-operation of the whole
village, but the amount of labour involved in actually handling
water is not very great. Gravity does most of the work.
The planning and supervision of the irrigation system is
more important for its efficient operation than the manual
labour.

2. *The scale of the hydraulic works determines forms of social
organization.*—This hypothesis can be divided into two aspects.
The absolute size of the irrigation system in relation to the
society using it is not dealt with decisively by Wittfogel. To
make correlations on this basis would require statistical data
which are not now available. If the Sonjo irrigation system
were to be ranked on a scale of absolute size it would undoubtedly be located in the lower part of the scale. Because of
its relatively small size the system has no need for a hierarchy
of officials and a bureaucracy to administer it, such as Wittfogel
describes for hydraulic societies in general (Wittfogel 1957 :
303 ff.), and this major aspect of his theory has to be disregarded. The Sonjo *wenamiji* combine in one office the roles of
ruler and primitive bureaucrat. A second way of applying the
criterion of size is in relation to the minimum independent unit
of the irrigation system. In the Sonjo villages the minimum
unit of irrigation involves the whole village. On the other hand,
there is no connexion between the systems of the different
villages so that no larger unit of irrigation exists. Assuming,
with Wittfogel, that the irrigation system is coterminous with
the political system of a hydraulic society, from these data
alone we might predict that the Sonjo village would be the
basic political unit of the society, and that is indeed what we

have actually found. If the sources of irrigation water for a single village—the streams and springs—were dispersed and unconnected, we might expect a different form of political organization, with perhaps clans, or whatever subgroup exploited the separate irrigation systems, constituting the basic political communities.

3. *Arid, semi-arid, and humid types of hydraulic environments should be distinguished*.—In a sociological context, the Sonjo environment should be classified as 'arid', for irrigation is not just a supplement, as in 'semi-arid' environments, or an alternative as in 'humid' environments, but is a necessary method for their existence as a sedentary, agricultural society. Thus irrigation and the water required for it are among the absolute values of the society. As we might expect from the surpassing ecological importance of irrigation, the social structure is centred on the irrigation system and much of the religious mythology and ritual relates to irrigation water. A conclusion which might be drawn from this is that irrigation *per se* need not result in a social system like that of the Sonjo; this could only be expected if climatic and environmental conditions were the same.

4. Of the three paramount characteristics of *hydraulic economy* distinguished by Wittfogel, the most important in his view (and the only one which will be discussed here) is that which *involves a specific type of division of labour*. In testing the Sonjo for this characteristic it is convenient to distinguish two aspects. In the first place the constructing and repairing of the physical framework of the irrigation system—the canals and sluices—require the unified labour of the whole village. The planning and supervising of this construction implies leadership with authority and special knowledge. A second aspect of the division of labour concerns the operation of the irrigation system. For the system to operate efficiently there must be close co-ordination of the work of all the men who use the water and agreement as to the principles of division. Since water is a valuable and at times scarce commodity, the users are competing for it against one another, and this competition might threaten to destroy the necessary co-ordination unless the whole system were controlled and regulated by a firm central authority. Therefore a group such as the *wenamiji* facilitates the operation of the hydraulic economy of the Sonjo. This close co-ordination and

M

central control required by the irrigation system distinguishes Sonjo agriculture from that of their non-irrigating neighbours.

5. *Control of irrigation and political leadership are identified in hydraulic societies.*—The data presented in chapters IV and VIII demonstrated the validity of this generalization for Sonjo society. We found that in each village a council of elders, called *wenamiji*, possesses authority to formulate rules for the use of irrigation water, to grant irrigation rights to individuals or to withhold these rights, and to regulate the operation of the system. The same *wenamiji* are the political rulers of the village with powers to issue orders and constitute themselves a court of law. These powers derive mainly from the control of irrigation: the threat of refusing irrigation water is an effective sanction in securing obedience. As the recognized village leaders, the *wenamiji* have control of the warrior classes which in turn support the rulers with physical force if needed. A major part of the present study has been devoted to describing the systems of irrigation control and of political leadership and investigating their correlation.

6. *The dominant religion is attached to the hydraulic régime and does not tolerate competing cults.*—Sonjo religion is remarkably uniform in that the basic myths and ritual are accepted at all the villages. While the role of the priests in the political organization of the tribe is not entirely clear from available data, they are definitely subordinate to the *wenamiji* in matters of political authority. The *wenamiji* themselves are sanctioned in their power by a mythological charter. Moreover they take leading parts in religious ritual and have close liaison with the priests, all of which attaches them closely to the tribal religion. As to the existence of cults which might compete with the dominant religion, we have seen that other common Bantu cults are weak or absent among the Sonjo. There is no special cult of rainmaking, and diviners or medicine men supposed to possess supernatural powers are not found. The cult of ancestral spirits is weak and limited to the small lineage group. Witchcraft is virtually absent from the tribe, though there is evidence that as recently as thirty years ago it was a thriving cult involving serious quarrels and heavy fines. Thus in the field of religion there is general agreement between Wittfogel's hypothesis and the Sonjo situation.

Irrigation-based societies have up to now received so little attention from social scientists that students dealing with this type of society must be grateful to Wittfogel for tackling the problem head-on. The six hypotheses which I abstracted from his writings were of considerable value to me in analysing my field material; they deserve further testing in other studies of societies with irrigation economies. It is not my purpose here to attempt an appraisal of Wittfogel's broad theory concerning the effect of irrigation on the political history of mankind. Many of his detailed hypotheses and assertions are quite inapplicable to the Sonjo; these I pass over in silence. However, it may be appropriate to discuss briefly his main thesis: namely, that hydraulic societies inevitably develop despotic types of government. He leaves us with no doubt that this kind of political system is undesirable.

In the last analysis, hydraulic government is government by intimidation.
Terror is the inevitable consequence of the rulers' resolve to uphold their own and not the people's rationality optimum. (Wittfogel 1957 : 137)

Can the Sonjo *wenamiji* be said to practise *intimidation* and *terror* for the sake of upholding their own power and selfish interests? These words imply the arbitrary exercise of power beyond what is justified by the laws and norms of the society. This is not the picture that I obtained of political life in a Sonjo village. The political authority of the Sonjo rulers is undoubtedly greater than those of other Bantu tribes in the immediate region: this is an important point in my analysis. But this authority is accepted by the people as valid and authentic; it is entirely in harmony with the prevailing customs, laws, myths, and ritual of the society. The ecological adjustment of the Sonjo, as compared with their neighbours who do not practise irrigation, requires closer organization of the society and more centralized authority for supervising economic activities. Considered in its ecological context, the political power of the Sonjo rulers could hardly be judged as 'despotic', even by strict standards of a democratic ideology. If we look only a little beyond the immediate neighbours of the Sonjo, we find

M*

in the non-irrigating Ganda and other interlacustrine kingdoms far more despotism and rigidity of class structure than among the hydraulic Sonjo.

In short, Wittfogel's main thesis finds little support from Sonjo data. If, as he insists, the large hydraulic societies of history inevitably develop despotic governments, the factor or factors responsible for this condition must arise in a later stage of ecological and social development than the Sonjo have reached. His attempt to demonstrate from ethnographic data that his theory of despotism is univerally applicable among hydraulic societies, large and small, is unconvincing. Among the traditional societies of Africa, and I dare say among tribal societies everywhere, despotism is a characteristic that seems to vary independently of the practice of irrigation.

A SIMPLIFIED MODEL OF SONJO SOCIETY

In final summary, I shall select out what have appeared to be the most essential structural features and with them attempt a concise description of Sonjo social structure viewed in ecological and historical perspective. As a theoretical framework upon which to construct this simplified model, I find it useful to employ Durkheim's concept of two contrasting types of social structure—the 'segmental type' based on 'mechanical solidarity', and the 'organized type' based on 'organic solidarity' (Durkheim 1947 : 174–90). The segmental type of structure is the earliest, according to Durkheim, and it tends to be progressively 'effaced' as the organized type develops. Thus the two types fully developed are not normally found in the same society, but segmental features do not completely disappear with the development of the organized type; traces of them persist.

In a Sonjo village the segmental principle is embodied in the clans. Although these are tied together by bonds of kinship and intermarriage and by common culture and language, their political relations with one another are essentially mechanical and result mainly from their territorial contiguity. Now in some ecological situations such mechanical relations between major units might be enough to ensure the survival of the society as a going concern. If we conceive of the Sonjo as inhabiting a region where irrigation was not necessary for cultivation, it is not difficult on the basis of comparative ethnology to imagine that land tenure could be entirely controlled by the clans and that the ecological situation would not require any higher form of political organization; and, as I shall suggest later, this may have been the picture of Sonjo society in an earlier period. However, if the ecological circumstances remain unchanged for a long period of time, the tendency is probably for these major units of such a society to become subdivided into lineages and sublineages. That is, a simple *segmental* society is transformed into a *segmentary* society of the type that has recently received a good deal of study.[1] Durkheim selected population growth as a major factor in bringing about the change from segmental to organized types of society. But increase in population size and density alone might also result in the development of a segmentary form of society. The resources of a Sonjo village set a definite limit to population size, and this may have inhibited the process of internal segmentation of the clans.

The 'organized' principle (in Durkheim's sense) is manifest in the unified village government consisting in the ruling group, whose political powers are derived on the one hand from its control of irrigation water and on the other from the religious ideology subscribed to by the whole society, and the system of classes which extend horizontally through the village, cutting across territorial and segmental subdivisions, and defined in terms of irrigation rights. The system of warrior classes is also consonant with an 'organized' type of social structure. Thus both of Durkheim's types are present in a Sonjo village, but they are unequal in strength. The 'organized' principle is strong and the 'segmental' principle is weak. I suggest that this disparity in the two principles can be explained by the ecological adaptation of the tribe. In further discussing this problem I shall substitute the term 'village government' for 'organized type' and 'clans' for 'segmental type'.

First let us review briefly the salient points concerning these two major structural elements. The clans are unilineal descent groups practising exogamy and are territorially localized. Each clan possesses a leader, but his authority is only directed

---

[1] Cf. Middleton and Tait 1958. The distinction between *segmental* and *segmentary* is discussed on page 8, note 1.

inwardly to the members of the clan; he does not represent the clan to the outside world and has no political dealings with other clans or with the village as a whole. He has power to adjudicate in disputes and to enforce norms which concern only the clan. The concerns of the clan, however, embrace only a small part of the total behaviour and interests of individuals. Therefore, properly to understand a clan we must take note of its negative features—the functions which it does not perform but which it might conceivably do. The clan has no control over productive resources; it controls house sites, which have considerable economic value, but the productive activities of agriculture, stock raising, and honey gathering are independent of any direct control by the clan. Except for the special case of the priests, the clan does not confer special status on its members: all significant rights and privileges of individuals are acquired elsewhere and not through membership in the clan. The clans take little part in the religious system of the village. An apparent exception to this statement is the existence of sacred springs which are associated mythologically and ritually with some of the clans. These associations suggest that at one time the clans may have performed significant religious functions, but at present the sacred springs are thoroughly integrated into the central cult of the whole society and their association with clans is largely nominal.

When the internal organization of a Sonjo clan is examined, we find a lack of definite structure. The clan is not systematically divided into lineage segments, but is essentially an aggregate of families and small lineage groups. The composition and size of the lineage group is determined mainly by the gerontocratic rules governing ownership of wealth and family authority. Although the principal forms of wealth—fields, livestock, and beehives—may be divided among adult sons while their father is still alive, the full rights of ownership remain with the father. These customs bind the sons together and to their father until his death. When relatives have no longer any mutual economic interest the bonds between them are weak. Genealogical knowledge is too shallow to produce an alignment of lineage groups into larger lineages. The bonds between clan-mates are essentially those of neighbours. Owing to the absence of an ancestor cult involving the whole clan or any other clan cult, these bonds are devoid of mystical quality. Even the belief in common biological descent of clan members is not an essential feature. Thus the bonds of clan membership may be broken, as in the divorce of a woman and her remarriage to a man of a different clan, in which case her children go with her, breaking relations with the clan of their birth. Such children then become members of their stepfather's clan, thus demonstrating that membership can be acquired in other ways than by birth into the group. As a test of the structural strength of clans, I suggested in the last chapter that we apply Firth's criterion and imagine Sonjo society as existing without clans—that is, without a belief in common unilineal descent. In that case there would be little change necessary in the social structure; the functions now served by clans could be equally well carried out by wards, with the single important exception of exogamy.

If Durkheim's explanation of population growth fails to account for the present social structure, then what is the basic reason that the Sonjo clans are weak and lacking in dynamic functions while the central government is strong and sharply structured? A similar question was investigated by Fallers (1956) in a study of the Soga of Uganda. That society possesses corporate lineages and also an organization of centralized government. Fallers found structural antagonism between these two principles of social organization. From his study of Soga society, and also from a consideration of other Interlacustrine tribes of East Africa, he concludes that 'the simultaneous structuring of authority within a society in terms of both corporate lineages and the state [is] productive of strain and instability' (p. 227). He found evidence of this strain and instability, among other places, in the personalities of individuals who had conflicting roles in lineage and state structures. 'One consequence of this instability . . . was . . . vulnerability to Western penetration' (p. 17). But despite this antagonism of structural elements and the resulting strains, Soga society was evidently able to maintain itself, and still does, as a going concern. This suggests that the ecological situation of that society permitted the development of these structural strains: tensions are not always and in all respects socially deleterious, but may sometimes enhance the economic effectiveness of a society.

Sonjo society, like that of the Soga, possesses corporate lineages and centralized government, but unlike Soga society it is free of conspicuous strains and instability and has been notably resistant to Western penetration. One reason for this, I suggest, is that structural strain and instability are incompatible with the ecological adaptation of the Sonjo. The successful operation of the irrigation system, upon which Sonjo society is dependent, requires the close co-operation of the men day after day. It requires minute planning and continual supervision. Authority must be unified and loyalties must be undivided, for any overt social conflict might disrupt the operation of the irrigation system and cause irreparable damage to crops. Thus, in stating the necessary social conditions imposed by the ecological adaptation of the Sonjo we define the main features of the social structure that actually exists—an 'organized' type of structure with centralized government whose essential structural parts are non-segmental. A political community if it has much size tends to be subdivided into territorial sub-units which serve definite social needs as 'neighbourhoods' but which need not be politically active. The Sonjo wards constitute such neighbourhoods.

If the Sonjo village can thus be adequately explained in terms of structure and function without reference to the clans as unilineal descent groups (because they serve no essential function in the total situation of ecological adaptation) how are we to account for the presence of clans? I have already suggested an answer to this with the hypothesis that the clans were formerly stronger than at present and that they then served essential social functions that are now lost. This hypothesis involves an attempt at historical reconstruction. But for that matter, any statement as to social adaptation has historical implications: to say that the institutions of a society are adapted to a certain manner of livelihood is to imply that those institutions were different before the present mode of livelihood was adopted and that they changed in response to ecological needs. In the absence of any need for them, the Sonjo clans could hardly have come into existence under the present ecological conditions of the society; but if they were already in existence before the Sonjo developed their irrigation economy, then they might well be expected to survive in attenuated form. I suggest that this is what happened and that the survival has been aided by the fact that the clans conveniently coincided with territorial subdivisions which were necessary but had no need for a lineage basis: this would imply that the Sonjo clans are in process of transformation into non-lineage wards.

If we accept Fallers's generalization about the structural antagonism between corporate lineages and centralized government and the instability and strain resulting when both are present in the same society, my hypothesis can be summarized in the form of a syllogism: Corporate lineages and centralized government existing together produce instability; instability is incompatible with the hydraulic economy of the Sonjo; therefore, in order for successful adaptation to take place, the antagonistic element least adaptive to the ecological situation (the clans) had to give way to the element best adapted to this situation (the central government).

REFERENCES CITED

BAKER, E. C. – 1949. 'History of the Wasegeju', *Tanganyika Notes and Records*, No. 27.

BAUMANN, OSCAR – 1894. *Durch Masailand zur Nilquelle*. Berlin.

BEECH, M. W. H. – 1911. *The Suk*. Oxford, Clarendon Press.

BERNARDI, B. – 1959. *The Mugwe, a Failing Prophet*. London, Oxford University Press *for* the International African Institute.

BRAIDWOOD, ROBERT J. – 1953. *The Near East and the foundations of civilization*. Condon Lectures. Eugene, Oregon, Oregon State System of Higher Education.

CHILDE, V. GORDON – 1946. *What happened in history*. New York, Penguin Books.
1953. *New light on the most ancient East*. New York, F. A. Praeger.

DUNDAS, CHARLES – 1924. *Kilimanjaro and its people*. London, Witherby.

DURKHEIM, E. – 1947. *The division of labor in society*. Glencoe, Illinois, The Free Press.

EAST AFRICA ROYAL COMMISSION – 1955. East Africa Royal Commission 1953–1955 report. London, H.M.S.O.

EISENSTADT, S. N. – 1956. *From generation to generation*. Glencoe, Illinois, The Free Press.

ELIKANA; ELIUFOO, S. N.; and SALEMA, H. – 1952. *Wasonjo na jinsi walivyopewa Agano Jipya*. Lutheran Church of Tanganyika.

EVANS-PRITCHARD, E. E. – 1940. *The Nuer*. Oxford, Clarendon Press.

FALLERS, LLOYD A. – 1956. *Bantu bureaucracy*. Cambridge, Heffers.

FINCH, F. G. – 1957. 'Hambageu, some additional notes on the God of the Wasonjo', *Tanganyika Notes and Records*, No. 47 & 48 : 203–8.

FIRTH, RAYMOND – 1951. *Elements of social organization*. London, Watts.

174 REFERENCES CITED

FISCHER, A. G. – 1884. 'Report of a journey in the Masai country', *Proceedings of the Royal Geographical Society* **6** : 76–83.

FORDE, C. DARYLL – 1946. *Habitat, economy and society* (Fifth edition). London, Methuen and Co.

FORTES, MEYER – 1936. 'Ritual festivals and social cohesion in the hinterland of the Gold Coast', *American Anthropologist* **38** : 590–604.
1945. *The dynamics of clanship among the Tallensi.* London, Oxford University Press.

FORTES, MEYER, and EVANS-PRITCHARD, E. E. – 1940. *African political systems.* London, Oxford University Press *for* International Institute of African Languages and Cultures.

FOSBROOKE, H. A. – 1953. 'A brief review of archeological remains in Tanganyika', *Tanganyika Notes and Records*, No. 33 : 63.
1955. 'Hambageu, the god of the Wasonjo', *Tanganyika Notes and Records*, No. 35 : 38–43.
1955a. 'The defence measures of certain tribes in North-Eastern Tanganyika, Part IV: Mbugwe flats and Sonjo scarps', *Tanganyika Notes and Records*, No. 39 : 1–11.
1956. 'The Masai age-grade system as a guide to tribal chronology', *African Studies*, **14** : 188–206.
1957. 'Early iron age sites in Tanganyika relative to traditional history', in *Third Pan-African Congress on Prehistory*, J. D. Clark (Ed.), London, Chatto and Windus.

FOX, D. STORRS – 1930. 'Further notes on the Masai of Kenya Colony', *Journal of the Royal Anthropological Institute*, **60** : 447–65.

FUSTEL DE COULANGES, N. D. – 1956. *The ancient city.* Garden City, New York, Doubleday and Company. (First published 1864.)

GLUCKMAN, MAX – 1955. *Custom and Conflict in Africa.* Glencoe, Illinois, The Free Press.

GRANT, H. ST. J. – 1953. Footnote in 'Hambageu, the god of the Wasonjo', H. A. Fosbrooke, *Tanganyika Notes and Records*, No. 33 : 40.

GRAY, ROBERT F. – 1960. 'Sonjo bride-price and the question of African "wife purchase" ', *American Anthropologist*, **62** : 34–57.

GRIFFITHS, J. E. S. – 1940. 'Notes on land tenure and land rights among the Sonjo of Tanganyika Territory', *Tanganyika Notes and Records*, No. 9.

GUTHRIE, MALCOLM – 1948. *The classification of the Bantu languages*. London, Oxford University Press *for* the International African Institute.

GUTMANN, BRUNO – 1926. *Das recht der Dschagga*. München.

HENNING, R. O. – 1951. *African morning*. London, Chatto and Windus.

HOEBEL, E. A. – 1954. *The law of primitive man*. Cambridge, Massachusetts, Harvard University Press.

HUNTINGFORD, G. W. B. – 1931. 'Ancient roads and dikes in Kenya Colony', *Man* **31** : 45.

JAEGER, FRITZ – 1913. 'Das hochland der reisenkrater (Teil II)', *Mitteilungen aus den Deutschen Schutzgebieten*, No. 8.

JOHNSTON, H. H. – 1919. *Comparative study of the Bantu and Semi-Bantu languages* (Vol. I). Oxford, Clarendon Press.

KOENIG, O. – 1951. 'The ancient wells of Ngassumat in South Masailand', *Tanganyika Notes and Records*, No. 31 : 53–4.

LANGHANS – 1897. 'Langhans Deutscher kolonial-atlas', No. 20, *Ost-Afrikanisches Schutzgebiet* in 4 blattern.

LEAKEY, L. S. B. – 1930. 'Some notes on the Masai of Kenya Colony', *Journal of the Royal Anthropological Society*, **60** : 185–210.
1935. 'Preliminary report on examination of the Engaruka ruins', *Tanganyika Notes and Records*, No. 1 : 57–60.

LINTON, RALPH – 1936. *The study of man*. New York, Appleton-Century Co.

MERTON, ROBERT K. – 1949. *Social theory and social structure*. Glencoe, Illinois, The Free Press.

MIDDLETON, JOHN – 1953. 'The Kikuyu and Kamba of Kenya', *Ethnographic survey of Africa, East Central Africa*, Part V. London, International African Institute.

MIDDLETON, JOHN, and TAIT, DAVID – 1958. *Tribes without rulers, studies in African segmentary systems*. London, Routledge and Kegan Paul.

PAVER, B. G. – 1957. *Zimbabwe cavalcade*. London, Cassell.

PRINS, A. H. J. – 1953. *East African age-class systems*. Groningen, Djakarta, J. B. Wolters.

RADCLIFFE-BROWN, A. R. – 1929. 'Age organization terminology', *Man* 29 : 21.
1933. 'Primitive law', *Encyclopedia of the Social Sciences.*
1940. 'Preface', in *African political systems,* M. Fortes and E. E. Evans-Pritchard (Eds.), London, Oxford University Press *for* the International African Institute.
1952. *Structure and function in primitive society.* Glencoe, Illinois, The Free Press.

SCHAPERA, I. – 1956. *Government and politics in tribal societies.* London, Watts.

SELIGMAN, C. G. – 1957. *The races of Africa.* London, Oxford University Press.

SIMENAUER, E. – 1955. 'The miraculous birth of Hambageu, hero-god of the Sonjo', *Tanganyika Notes and Records,* No. 38 : 23–30.

STEWARD, JULIAN H. – 1949. 'Cultural causality and law', *American Anthropologist,* **51**: 1–27.
1953. 'Evolution and process', in *Anthropology today,* A. L. Kroeber and others (Eds.), Chicago, University of Chicago Press.
1955. *Theory of culture change: the methodology of multilinear evolution.* Urbana, University of Illinois Press.

STEWARD, JULIAN H. *et al.* – 1955. *Irrigation civilization: a comparative study.* Washington, Pan American Union.

SUMMERS, ROGER – 1958. *Inyanga, prehistoric settlements in Southern Rhodesia.* Cambridge University Press.

WAKEFIELD, T. – 1870. 'Routes of native caravans from the coast to the interior of Eastern Africa, chiefly from information given by Sadi Bin Ahedi, a native of a district near Gazi, in Udigo, a little north of Zanzibar', *Journal of the Royal Geographical Society,* **40** : 303–39.

WEBER, MAX – 1958. *From Max Weber: essays in sociology* (translated and edited by H. H. Gerth and C. W. Mills). New York, Oxford University Press.

WIDTSOE, JOHN A. – 1920. *The principles of irrigation practice.* New York, the Macmillan Co.

WILSON, G. E. H. – 1932. 'Ancient civilization of the Rift Valley', *Man* 32 : 250–7.

WINTER, E. H. – 1956. *Bwamba—a structural-functional analysis of a patrilineal society*. Cambridge, Heffers.

WITTFOGEL, KARL A. – 1955. 'Developmental aspects of hydraulic societies', in *Irrigation civilizations: a comparative study*, Julian H. Steward *et al.*
1956. 'The hydraulic civilizations', in *Man's role in changing the face of the earth*, William L. Thomas, Jr. (Ed.), Chicago, University of Chicago Press.
1957. *Oriental despotism, a comparative study of total power*. New Haven, Yale University Press.

WORSLEY, P. M., and RUMBERGER, J. P. – 1949. 'Remains of an earlier people in Uhehe', *Tanganyika Notes and Records*, No. 27 : 42–6.

INDEX

Printed by
The Anchor Press, Ltd.,
Tiptree, Essex